The Immoderate Past

The Immoderate Past
The Southern Writer and History

by

C. HUGH HOLMAN

Turn your eyes to the immoderate past,
Turn to the inscrutable infantry rising
Demons out of the earth—they will not last.
—Allen Tate

The 1976 Lamar Lectures at Wesleyan College

The University of Georgia Press
Athens

Paperback edition, 2008
© 1977 by the University of Georgia Press
Athens, Georgia 30602
www.ugapress.org
All rights reserved
Printed digitally in the United States of America

The Library of Congress has cataloged
the hardcover edition of this book as follows:

Library of Congress Cataloging-in-Publication Data

Holman, C. Hugh (Clarence Hugh), 1914–1981.
    The immoderate past: the southern writer and history /
by C. Hugh Holman.
    ix, 118 p. ; 23 cm.
    ISBN 0-8203-0419-0
    Includes index.
    Bibliography: p. [111]-113.
    1. American fiction—Southern States—History and criticism.
2. Historical fiction, American—History and criticism. 3. History
in literature. 4. Southern States—In literature. I. Title. II. Series:
The Lamar lectures (Wesleyan College); 1976.
PS261.H64   1977   813'.03   76-58439

Paperback ISBN-13: 978-0-8203-3357-1
ISBN-10: 0-8203-3357-3

Contents

	Preface	vii
1.	The Southern Writer and the Rorschach Test of History	1
2.	"The Tory Camp is Now in Sight": The Past as Apologia	13
3.	"Time ... The Sheath Enfolding Experience": The Past as a Way of Life	38
4.	"To Grieve on Universal Bones": The Past as Burden	66
5.	"The Cosmic Clock of History"	93
	Notes	102
	A Note on Sources	111
	Index	115

To

The Memory of

GREGORY LANSING PAINE
(1877-1950)
Who showed me the problem

Preface

THESE essays were delivered, in slightly abbreviated form, as the 18th Annual Eugenia Dorothy Blount Lamar Lecture Series, at Wesleyan College, in Macon, Georgia, on April 7 and 8, 1976. They are presented here in expanded and documented form, and with the addition of the concluding essay, which grew out of discussions at Wesleyan.

The invitation to give this series of lectures encouraged me to bring into some order matters about southern writing and its relation to the past which have been a persistent concern of mine for more than a quarter of a century. In these essays I have tried to organize materials around a unifying concept of the southerner's view of the past and time, as opposed to the received standard American view of the present and space.

I know that I have dealt with large and only casually defined issues, and that the conclusions that I have reached from reading many southern novels over many years and studying the qualities of the southern mind for half a century are asserted rather than demonstrated. These faults are inherent in the lecture format. I have tried to minimize them to some degree by giving fairly detailed treatment to a few books which I use as representative, including William Gilmore Simms's Revolutionary romances, Ellen Glasgow's *The Battle-Ground,* Allen Tate's *The Fathers,* and several of Robert Penn Warren's works.

In the Foreword to his Jefferson Lecture in the Humanities, *Democracy and Poetry,* Robert Penn Warren said, ". . . behind almost every paragraph lies some unargued assumption which may be objected to. . . . All I can hope, for both the conscious and the unconscious assumptions, is that, even if they are not acceptable to a reader, they may exhibit some sort of coherence, some internal consistency." I echo this southern master of the historical imagination, and only add my conviction that, whether the reader accepts my assumptions or not, the data here does point to a special relationship of the southern novelist with history.

I am grateful to Dean Oscar C. Page, of Wesleyan College, for inviting me to deliver the lectures and for his assistance in their publication. The occasion of their presentation was very happy and rewarding for me. A number of the Wesleyan people went far beyond the call of duty to make my stay in Macon pleasant. In addition to Dean Page—truly a tower of strength—I should like to acknowledge the special kindnesses of President W. Earl Strickland; Dr. Earl Bargainnier, chairman of the English Department; Dr. Leah Strong, chairman of American Studies; and Dr. Harry Gilmer.

In the process of preparing these essays, longer statements than were practical for delivery as lectures evolved. One of these, "Ellen Glasgow and History: *The Battle-Ground*," was published in *Prospects 2*, edited by Jack Salzman (New York: Burt Franklin, 1976). Another, "William Gilmore Simms's Changing Views of Loyalism in the Revolution," appeared in the Fall 1976 issue of the *Mississippi Quarterly*. Two essays on Simms's novels *The Forayers* and *Eutaw* will be published in the Proceedings of a Conference on Simms and the Revolution, held in Charleston, May 6–8, 1976. So the invitation has proved unusually fruitful for me.

Without the research made possible by a John Simon Guggenheim Memorial Fellowship, the fundamental conception would never have been articulated or the

Preface

study have been possible that put flesh—however scanty—on that skeleton. This little book is another earnest of the debt I owe that foundation and its president, Gordon N. Ray.

As usual my debts to my graduate students at the University of North Carolina at Chapel Hill have been great, particularly to Jeffrey Steinbrink, now of Franklin and Marshall College, whose explorations of history and fiction I have found very stimulating. My debt to my colleague Louis D. Rubin, Jr., for information, encouragement, and that rarest of the flowers of friendship, frank criticism, is great for this work as it has been for many things. To Professor Robert D. Jacobs, of Georgia State University, I am indebted for illuminating suggestions made on hearing me read an early draft of what became chapters 1 and 5. For numerous services performed with grace, skill, and dispatch, I am once more in the debt of Mrs. Dinah S. Lloyd. My debts are especially great to my wife, who patiently endured the months of effort which this little book represents.

C. Hugh Holman

Chapel Hill, North Carolina

1

The Southern Writer and the Rorschach Test of History

> ... we are like the scientist fumbling with a tooth and a thigh bone to reconstruct for a museum some great, stupid beast extinct with the ice age. Or we are like the louse-bit nomad who finds, in a fold of land between his desert and the mountains, the ruin of parapets and courts, and marvels what kind of men had held the world before him. But at least we have the record: the tooth and thigh bone, or the kingly ruins. —Robert Penn Warren, *World Enough and Time*
>
> For every Southern boy fourteen years old, not once but whenever he wants it, there is the instant when it's still not yet two o'clock on that July afternoon in 1863, the brigades are in position behind the rail fence, the guns are laid and ready in the woods and the furled flags are already loosened to break out and Pickett himself with his long oiled ringlets and his hat in one hand probably and his sword in the other looking up the hill waiting for Longstreet to give the word and it's all in the balance....
> —William Faulkner, *Intruder in the Dust*

THE IMAGINATION of the southerner for over one hundred and seventy-five years has been historical. The imagination of the Puritans was essentially typological, catching fire as it saw men and events as types of Christian principles. The imagination of the New England romantics was fundamentally symbolic, translating material objects into ideal forms and ideas. The southerner has always had his imaginative faculties excited by events in time and has found the most profound truths of the present and the future in the interpretation of the past.

Jack Burden, in Robert Penn Warren's *All the King's Men*, says, "Reality is not a function of the event as event, but of the relationship of that event to past, and future, events. . . . the reality of an event, which is not real in itself, arises from other events."[1] Such an attitude does not require explanation in the South, but it has appeared infrequently in what is often called the mainstream of American thought and writing. History—the pattern events make in time—has had little meaning in the larger nation, but it has been a persistent and obsessive element in southern thought. One of Saul Bellow's characters says, "When I say American I mean uncorrected by the main history of human suffering."[2] The South has not escaped such correction, and its past is a constant reminder and explanation of its suffering.

The tendency to see events and people at least as linked steps in a continuing process if not in terms of large overarching meanings is something that has rarely excited the American imagination until this century. Only recently, when many of the promises of the American experience are contradicted or questioned by the events which grew out of them, have we, as a nation, begun to turn our eyes backward—whether as New Historians or as old ones—to the sequence of event and causation which produced the world in which we live. Most Americans were for a long time like Nick Carraway in Scott Fitzgerald's *The Great Gatsby*, who said as he looked at Long Island in the moonlight, "I became aware of the old island here that flowered once for Dutch sailors' eyes—a fresh, green breast of the new world. Its vanished trees . . . had once pandered in whispers to the last and greatest of all human dreams; for a transitory enchanted moment man must have held his breath in the presence of this continent . . . face to face for the last time in history with something commensurate to his capacity for wonder."[3]

Fitzgerald, in this passage, is looking back to the past of Long Island and of America by an exercise of his imagination, but the imaginative process which he assumes for his Dutch sailors was of a different sort; it was an imagination not of the past but of the future, and in this respect the sailors were truly American. Their world was new; their beginnings were fresh beginnings; their experiment was an experiment in the future; they were challenged by the green earth to write history on a land without a past. Such fresh beginnings were generally true of the settlement of most of the continent outside the South. New England, which in many respects has dominated the intellectual life of America to the present, was settled by people cutting their ties with an old and disliked European past and constructing on a true tabula rasa a New Jerusalem, a City on a Hill, patterned in fresh ways and looking toward a different hope of history and the operation of different forces in its future.

It was not so with the groups who settled the coastal plains of the southern Atlantic coast of North America. Whether there was cavalier blood in their veins or not, there were certainly cavalier ideas firmly implanted in their minds, and almost from the beginning they began to reconstruct upon the coastal soil of Virginia and the Carolinas a world modeled in many ways on that which they had left. They were almost from the first concerned with English politics, English manners, and the Church of England. The great men of the eighteenth century in Virginia looked homeward to England for their education, for many of their friendships, and for inspiration, while the New Englander set his face in stony opposition to the thoughts and patterns of the world that he had left. William Byrd of Westover, in Virginia, whom Louis B. Wright has called "a proud and dandified colonial gentleman, eager to retain the good opinion of aristocratic friends in England,"[4] was a member of the Middle Temple, frequented the Inns of Court, and was elected to membership in the Royal Society.[5]

There is little doubt that the basic colonial experience,

aside from certain differences in climate and terrain, was much the same in the North and in the South. But how we see events as parts of historical patterns is a function not of facts but of what our imagination does with facts. As Reinhold Niebuhr once said:

Any interpretation of historical patterns and configurations raises the question whether the patterns, which the observer discerns, are "objectively" true or are imposed upon the vast stuff of history by his imagination. History might be likened to the confusion of spots on the cards used by psychiatrists in a Rorschach test. The patient is asked to report what he sees in these spots; and he may claim to find the outlines of an elephant, butterfly or frog. The psychiatrist draws conclusions from these judgments about the state of the patient's imagination rather than about the actual configuration of spots on the card.[6]

In the nineteenth century, although there were almost endless variations on them, through most of the Western world two ways of ordering the blots on the cards of history were dominant. One sees history as a process, a vast systematic movement through the dimension of time toward some at best vaguely recognizable goal. The Christian religion, which profoundly influenced Western thought in the modern world, always asserted such a view: History is the objective working out of the will or intention of God. The view of history as process is perhaps best represented in the nineteenth century by Georg Wilhelm Friedrich Hegel's *Philosophy of History,* in which history is seen as a record of the developing embodiment of the World-Spirit and is explained by the existence of a World-Process and The Self-Realizing Idea. History for Hegel was a vast drama in which man, responding to Reason, is the hero and in which a process of change and development was inevitable, realized in great, surging waves of change, and magnificent. Hegel's sentences ring with confidence: "The history of the world, therefore, presents us with a rational process." "It may be said of Universal History, that it is the exhibition of Spirit in the process of working out the knowledge of that which it is potentially." "The whole process of History . . . is directed to rendering this unconscious impulse a conscious one." "Historical men—*World-Historical Individuals*—are those in whose aims such a general principle [of Truth] lies." "Universal History exhibits the *gradation* in the development of that principle whose substantial *purport* is the consciousness of Freedom." "The life of the ever present Spirit is a circle of progressive embodiment." And being a devout Christian, Hegel concluded *The Philosophy of History:* "That the History of the World, with all the changing scenes which its annals present, is this process of development and the realization of Spirit—this is the true *Theodicaea*, the justification of God in History. Only *this* insight can reconcile Spirit with the History of the World—viz., that what has happened, and is happening every day, is not only not 'without God,' but is essentially His Work."[7] And this view of history as process had wide acceptance and application throughout the century, with Karl Marx being deeply indebted to it, though he prided himself on turning Hegel's dialectic upside down.[8]

The other way of viewing the blots on the cards of history is to deny vast overarching meanings and to find meaning in the subjective rather than, as Hegel had, in the realization of the subjective in the objective, "the means the World-Spirit uses for realizing its Idea."[9] The major thinkers of New England in the nineteenth century pursued in their way the ideal of a New World and a New Jerusalem and usually found it, not in an order of events but within the self. They early embraced a view of history as a record of the self. Emerson, for example, said, "The book, the college, the school of art, the institution of any kind, stop with some past utterance of genius. . . . They look backward and not forward. But genius looks forward: the eyes of man are set in his forehead, not in his hindhead: man hopes: genius creates."[10] And

Henry David Thoreau ended one of the half-dozen finest works produced in America in the nineteenth century with these words: "I do not say that John or Jonathan will realize all this; but such is the character of that morrow which mere lapse of time can never make to dawn. The light which puts out our eyes is darkness to us. Only that day dawns to which we are awake. There is more day to dawn. The sun is but a morning star."[11] James Russell Lowell, in 1844, warned against trusting "mouldy parchments" and urged his fellow New Englanders to

> Launch our Mayflower, and steer boldly through the desperate winter sea,
> Nor attempt the Future's portal with the Past's blood-rusted key.[12]

But of nineteenth-century thinkers, the one who most emphatically opposed the view of Hegel was Friedrich Nietzsche, who denied in embittered anger the existence of Hegelian historical process and saw Hegel's patterns of the past and of change as mind-forged manacles. There was, Nietzsche felt, eternal recurrence in the universe, but it was individual recurrence, and it denied, except within the individual, any pattern, any progression, or any process. Man, for Nietzsche, eternally suffers the traumas of birth and death, and reconciliation to this fate is his only salvation. His significant history is within himself and not outside, and it is the individual's action that matters. History he calls a disease. Man, he laments, "cannot learn to forget, but hangs on to the past: however far or fast he runs, that chain runs with him." "The past and the present," he says, "are one and the same, typically alike in all their diversity and forming together a picture of eternally present imperishable types of unchangeable value and significance." Contemptuously he declares Hegel's view of history a "heroic symphony . . . arranged for two flutes for the use of dreaming opium smokers."

And angrily he declares, "There has been no dangerous turning point in the progress of German culture in this century that has not been made more dangerous by . . . Hegelian philosophy." And he mockingly sums up Hegel's teachings about history as, "Forward then boldly, with the world-process, as workers in the vineyard of the Lord, for it is the process alone that can lead to redemption!"[13]

In the South, in contrast to the dominance in America of this Nietzschean attitude, a view of historical process and a sense of the crucial importance of the past has dominated the imagination, and there were many reasons for the South's Hegelian passion for historical process.

In the first third of the nineteenth century one of the great artistic influences throughout the Western world was the discovery by Sir Walter Scott that historical process lent itself with singular effectiveness to the construction of novels and romances. In the Waverley Novels Scott presented a fictional world firmly shaped by a sense of history as process and thus he added significantly to man's consciousness of himself as a being in history, as an actor in the dimension of time. To assert that from Scott's work stemmed for many readers a sense of man in history is not to try to claim for him great philosophical depth but rather to claim that he had an imagination fired by the sequence of events which makes process, by the evolution of the World-Spirit through action and opposition, by the progressive interaction of subjective and objective which is the Hegelian sense of process in the world. The Hungarian critic Georg Lukács has written brilliantly and authoritatively about Scott's classical embodiment of this Hegelian sense of history. No one can read Lukács's impressive study *The Historical Novel* with care and afterward dismiss Scott's romances as mere tinsel-coated derring-do. As Lukács says, "Scott endeavors to portray the struggles and antagonisms of history by means of characters who, in their psychology and destiny, always represent social trends and historical forces."[14] But there was no need to wait for a Hungarian Marxist to point this out, for in Scott's own time this quality in his work was sensed and valued. Coleridge, for example, saw the Waverley Novels as resting on "the contest between the two great living principles of social humanity: religious adherence to the past and the ancient, the desire and the admiration of permanance, on the one hand; and the passion for increase of knowledge, for truth, as the offspring of reason—in short, the mighty instincts of *progression* and *free agency*, on the other."[15] This conclusion is startlingly like one which the historian C. Vann Woodward and the novelists William Styron, Ralph Ellison, and Robert Penn Warren reached in a discussion of history and fiction in New Orleans in 1968, although they were certainly not intentionally echoing Coleridge or discussing Scott.[16]

Between 1814 and 1840 most of America, like most of the world, loved and read the Waverley Novels of Sir Walter Scott, who was the model for most American novelists.[17] James Fenimore Cooper, who was his most successful imitator in the New World, however, took out of the Scott formula what he regarded as the bondage of historical fact and replaced it with a single epic hero, Natty Bumppo, who always stood as a unique and ideal individual arrested between the forces of past and future in an eternal and westward moving Now.[18] Of Cooper's thirty-two novels only one, *Lionel Lincoln,* is a strictly historical novel in that it deals specifically and in detail with carefully reconstructed historical events. Hawthorne, who as a boy and a young man had loved Scott just this side of idolatry, by the middle 1840s saw him as a past influence to be turned against and declared that it was time that the worn-out mold of the Scott novel should be broken and thrown away.[19] When the rest of the nation in the 1840s and 1850s had set Scott aside as belonging to their unsophisticated youth, the South was still reading him in great quantity and buying his works by the freight-car loads down to the beginning of the Civil War,[20] which, you will recall, Mark Twain blamed on the "Sir Walter disease."[21]

Certainly the enormous popularity of the Waverley Novels and of the works of Scott's successors in the form, such as G.P.R. James and Harrison Ainsworth, helped to foster and inform the South's concern with history, but it was the unusual intensity of that concern which kept the South reading Scott and naming its towns, its homesteads, and its children for Scott's places and characters long after the rest of the nation had turned to other kinds of fiction.

There were a number of reasons, besides the influence of Scott, for the South's obsession with history and with theories about historical process. A primary one is the fact that the South was an agricultural region; in every agrarian culture there is a strong sense of family solidarity; kinship means much; and the family Bibles with their records of births and deaths, like the great ledgers in William Faulkner's "The Bear,"[22] are repositories in miniature of the history of a place, of a region, and of the world. Another is the fact that in the nineteenth century the agricultural staples of the South were cotton and tobacco, crops which rapidly deplete the soil. Early in the century the awareness of this worn-out soil contributed its significant, dampening bit to the sense of a past rather than a present or a future glory.[23] Edmund Ruffin in 1832 published perhaps his most important though by no means his most inflammatory piece of work, a small book entitled *An Essay on Calcareous Manures*. A part of its purpose was to improve agriculture and thus arrest the forced western migration of Tidewater planters.[24] Among the forces actively at work to create the large social and economic frame within which the events in William Styron's *The Confessions of Nat Turner* occurred were this depletion of the soil and the weakening of the economy in Tidewater Virginia. The golden age of Charleston was the eighteenth century. By the 1830s, not only were its great men shadowy memories, its commerce was suffering; and the economic history of the "City by the Sea" was one of efforts to link itself by rail to the retreating West.[25] When Williamsburg was reconstructed, it was rebuilt as it stood in the days of colonial Virginia. The state which prided itself for more than a century on being "The Mother of Presidents" was really the mother of early presidents. The intellectual life of Virginia, as Richard Beale Davis has effectively demonstrated, was an intellectual life peculiarly eighteenth century, which reached its flowering in the age of Thomas Jefferson.[26]

As soil depletion and population growth forced the South steadily to move westward, it forced it physically away from that part of the past which seemed to it beneficent, orderly, and with the qualities of magnificence, and thus the nineteenth-century South was bound emotionally to that lost world. The South was looking back to past glories and comparing its present unfavorably with a glorious past long before the Civil War. Hence there was a fundamentally conservative cast to the southern mind, a strong reverence for traditions, and something like Scott's Tory nostalgia for a lost good world.

A kind of golden-age primitivism is in the conservative southerner whether he be, in 1820, lamenting the days when there were giants strutting the streets of the seaport of Charleston, or whether he be, in 1875, remembering with imperfect but magnifying force the infinitely tall white columns of nonexistent plantation houses, or whether he be at Nashville, in the 1930s, opposing to the industrialism of the present world an agrarian order that never quite was on land or sea. The South's hunger for the past is deep rooted; it has always been passionate, and it has always been complex. That past has betrayed it, misled it, cozened it, and cuckolded it; and yet the involvement of the southerner with his history has remained intense and unremitting, equaled only by his passion for the land itself and not surpassed even by that.

While this is said it must also be added that in the South's obsession with history and with the past there have often been attempts to find in accounts of other cultures or in the earlier days of its own justifications for the sin that it has steadily committed against its darker-skinned brethren. Such a concern for history in the 1840s and 1850s could sometimes reach the ludicrous proportion of reconstructing the days of the Greek republic in order to demonstrate that a noble culture rested upon the mudsill of slavery. But whether the reasons are nostalgic, intellectually sound, or morally indefensible, the South through the nineteenth century and into the twentieth maintained a passionate interest in the past, had its imagination deeply stirred by the past, and found in the past a shape that has dominated its literary expression. In no other section of the country, I believe, can so obsessive a concern with the past, particularly a concern shaped by serious philosophical attempts to understand its shape, its forces, and its nature, be found.

If the South has been, as I have suggested, for the last one hundred and seventy-five years, the prisoner of its past, its mind has found in that imprisonment the materials out of which it has fashioned from time to time art of a very high order. Its concern with *what is* as a product of *what was* and the shaper of *what may be,* with history viewed as a process in which events are inexorably linked to each other in a broad shape, is so characteristic of many of its best minds that we can think of the South as a region passionately hungry for the meaning of the shape of its past and with a strong sense of the overarching process by which past becomes future. The eternal Now its individuals occupy has powerful links to a social world with elaborate patterns of causation and response, and these things have kept the imagination of its best writers occupied with the complex and public world.

The historical novel has been a principal means by which southern novelists have used the past to create serious exempla for their readers, and they have done it in differing ways at different times. It shall be our purpose in these essays to look at three of those ways: How writers before the Civil War used the classic form of the historical novel as Scott developed it to show how, during the American Revolution, the region contributed essentially to the making of the nation. How writers, emphasizing the novel of manners aspect of the realistic movement, set out to describe and define the texture and quality of the life of past ages. And, finally, how novelists have utilized modern experimental techniques to explore the problems of the historical South and the guilt we all inherit from our past.

2
"The Tory Camp Is Now in Sight": The Past as Apologia

> Who did not know ... that in the Revolution it was the South that had led in the fight for freedom, and freedom, therefore, was beyond all price? —Stark Young, *So Red the Rose*

> We had lost the Southern cause—the kind of country we had wanted, the sort of life we had created out of the earlier Revolution. —Ben Robertson, *Red Hills and Cotton*[1]

IN 1860, when the southern civilization of which William Gilmore Simms had been perhaps the most effective literary spokesman, was on the precipice over which it was to fall into dissolution, *De Bow's Review* published an essay on Simms praising him about as highly as a literary man can be praised. It declared, "Mr. Simms is yet in the meridian of his faculties—time, alone, can complete the fullness of his fame; and as the dawn was bright and full of promise, and the noon illuminated by the splendors of performance, the evening will catch the accumulated radiance, and plant among the fixed lights, the constellation that glitters to his genius."[2] He was, the anonymous writer asserted, one who reflects "the spirit and temper of Southern civilization; announces its opinions, illustrates its ideas, embodies its passions and prejudices, and betrays those delicate shades of thought, feeling, and conduct, that go to form the character, the stamp, the individuality of a people."[3] When this panegyric appeared, the bulk of Simms's important work had, ironically, already been done; and that work did, indeed, embody better than that of any other literary figure the aspirations, the ideals, and the attitudes of the Old South. By 1860 Simms had published twenty full-length novels—and thirteen of them had been historical—four histories, five biographies, and numerous pamphlets, reviews, and essays dealing with history. Clearly he saw history as the raw material of art and art as the most effective instructor of the people. Simms was, as William R. Taylor has declared, "the historical consciousness of the South."[4]

While most of the nation outside the South saw truth in terms of the perceptions, development, and lives of unique individuals, Simms saw truth primarily in terms of a sequence of past, present, and future, in which to know the past was essential for the comprehension of the present and projection into the future. As Simone Vauthier has said, in the best study of Simms's philosophy of time: "The interest in things past . . . was further encouraged . . . when he was a member of the Young America Movement by the desire to foster 'Americanism in literature' through the treatment of historical themes, which he often conceived of as historical events."[5] Simms declared, "It is through [history] that the past lives to the counselling and direction of the future, and if she breathe not the breath of life into its nostrils, the wires of the resurrectionists would vainly link together the ricketty skeleton which he disinters for posterity."[6] The "facts" of history, which in the nineteenth century were being pieced together by the new German historians, were for Simms so many scattered fragments of the irremediably lost fabric of human history. These facts may be all that we can know literally, but they assume meaning—that is, receive the breath of life into their nostrils—only when they have been assembled in a pattern meaningful to the present. He presupposed, as Hegel had, that there was a gradually unfolding meaning in the pattern of history, and he sought in history truths not only of the individual but of the race, not only of time but of eternity. He said, "The moral objects of the poet and the historian concern not the individual so much as the race,—are not simply truths of time, but truths of eternity."[7]

Simms saw the historical novel as the most successful form for a linkage of past, present, and future. Most American attempts to find meaning in the pattern of the national experience have been through movement in space—that is, through the recurring invasion and conquering of the frontier—a movement in which there is a steady repetition of events in time. Thus, in this view, as we move across space we find successive epochs in human history being replicated in constantly changing places.[8] This concept of the meaning of history is remarkably like Nietzsche's, in which history is the endless replication within individual lives of the common racial experiences. Not so with Simms or with most who find in history special meanings. For Simms saw a strong link between a love of land and place and a sense of change in time located upon that land and place, with the result that his form of truth was found in time not in geography. In this view, as in many other ways, this archetypical southerner almost from the beginning of his career was at variance with his national fellow novelists. James Fenimore Cooper, for example, in the Leatherstocking Tales repeated at five geographical stages the same essential event—that is, the conflict of the white man's culture with that of the Indian in the moment of most intense interaction. Yet Natty Bumppo is a figure not of the past or of the future but one who exists in the essential Now and hence one without history in time but with movement in space.

Though Simms was remarkably well-read in the history available to him—William R. Taylor declares that in

Simms's library at "Woodlands" he had over 12,000 volumes of material on American Revolutionary history[9]—he was suspicious of the ability of formal history ever to get at the essence of an experience or to uncover truth as a process in time, to him the essential nature of truth. Hence, for Simms the greatest source of historical truth is not in documents but in memory, in the oral traditions of a people. For him one of the principal sources of these oral traditions was his grandmother, Mrs. Jacob Gates, of whom he wrote: "My grandmother was an old lady who had been a resident of the seat of most frequent war in Carolina during the Revolution. She had fortunately survived the numberless atrocities which she was yet compelled to witness; and, a keen observer, with a strong memory, she had in store a thousand legends of that stirring period, which served to beguile me from sleep many and many a long winter night."[10] And writing of himself in the third person, he described the impression which such legends made upon him:

> He had his lessons at the knees of those who were young spectators in the grand panorama of our Revolution. . . . This was their favorite topic. . . . How the boy brooded over these narratives! . . . There was scarcely a personage, British or American, Whig or Loyalist—scarcely an event mournful or glorious—scarcely a deed, grand or savage—occurring in the history of the low country of South-Carolina, which has not been conned, for his benefit, at the writer's fireside, by venerable friends and loving kinswomen, now voiceless in the dust. . .
>
> [The Revolution] was made life-like to his imagination by personal histories, which appealed to his nearest affections and fondest sympathies.[11]

In defending the accuracy of his novel *Mellichampe*, he wrote of "the unquestionable records of history, and—in the regard of the novelist—the scarcely less credible testimonies of that venerable and moss-mantled Druid, Tradition."[12] His novel *The Partisan* had its origin, he says, in recollections of boyhood, as he visited the "now utterly decayed town of Dorchester," remembered his youthful rambles over the place, and recalled its "domestic chronicles, [heard] from the lips of one—now no more—who had been perfectly conversant with its local history, as with a large body of revolutionary and traditional history besides. Many of its little lessons were impressed upon my memory, and the fortunes of more than one of its families, of whom no record now remains, but that of the place of burial, were deeply scored upon my mind.... It was with the revival of old memories, and the wakening of new impulses and sentiments, that I rambled."[13]

With such memory as a primary source, the natural principal subject for Simms throughout his career was the American Revolutionary War. To that war he devoted a substantial amount of direct historical writing, including *The History of South Carolina, from Its First European Discovery to Its Erection into a Republic* (1840), *The Life of Francis Marion* (1844), *The Life of Nathanael Greene* (1849), and *South Carolina in the Revolutionary War: Being a Reply to Certain Misrepresentations and Mistakes of Recent Writers, in Relation to the Course and Conduct of This State* (1853). He wrote brief sketches of Greene, Charles Lee, Moultrie, Sumter, Gadsden, Huger, Pinckney, and Kosciusko for Griswold's *Washington and the Generals of the American Revolution*,[14] and he produced a number of pamphlets, essays, and reviews as well as public addresses on the Revolutionary War.

But in all such work he was bound by the limits of the demonstrable facts of history, and what he truly sought to do with the Revolution was, as Vauthier has wisely noted, to treat it as "the most flexible metaphor for his country's problem, the most telling image of what the South was not and ought to be, was and ought not to be."[15] Therefore, it was in his seven loosely connected novels dealing with the Revolutionary War in South Carolina from June 1780 until the summer of 1783 that Simms made the most effective use of the combination of memory, tradition, and formal history cast in the matrix of fiction which he was ever to make and perhaps the most ambitious single treatment in fiction of the American Revolution before this century.

These novels, written over a period of twenty years, form four distinct groups. The first group, consisting of *The Partisan* (1835) and *Mellichampe* (1836), strives to preserve the oral traditions of the Revolution before they fade from memory. He declared that in writing *The Partisan* his motive force had been "A sober desire for history—the unwritten, the unconsidered, but veracious history."[16] Both are essentially stories of vigorous action, in which brave warriors in Marion's brigade harass the British and the loyalists and begin to reopen the conflict between colony and mother country in South Carolina. That the Revolution in that colony was primarily a civil war fought with blood and terror between loyalists and rebels Simms clearly recognizes, and that the loyalists had an understandable if not defensible position he also recognizes, for he sees that the excessive actions of the patriots had driven many people into the loyalists' camp. In one sense these first two novels may be regarded as a plea for common sense and reason in dealing with people of all political persuasions.

The second group contains a single novel, *The Kinsmen*, better known as *The Scout;* it was published in 1841, after Simms had produced most of his novels dealing with the frontier in Georgia, Alabama, and Mississippi, such as *Richard Hurdis* and *Border Beagles. The Scout,* laid in the Up Country of South Carolina and centered on the siege of Fort Ninety-Six, emphasized, as Donald Davidson has pointed out, that the Revolutionary struggle in South Carolina was in essence a frontier conflict, marked by violence and unbridled lawlessness.[17]

Between 1842 and 1849, for several reasons but principally because the aftermath of the Panic of 1837 had so thoroughly depressed the market for fiction that it had become unprofitable, Simms had turned to biography, short fiction, and magazine editing.[18] Although he wrote much of his formal history and biography during this period, the Revolution did not figure in his fiction. When he returned to it as a fictional subject in 1849, as he began working on the novel *Katharine Walton,* his attitudes and impulses toward the Revolutionary War had undergone significant changes, and in that work he produced a historical novel of manners about life in Charleston under British rule. His emphasis had shifted from concern with the daring deeds of courageous young warriors to the intricacies of politics and the problems of mixed and uncertain loyalties. *Katharine Walton* is more like Thackeray's *Henry Esmond* than it is like Scott's *Waverley.* A novel that was a companion piece in many ways was published the following year under the title *The Sword and the Distaff* but better known as *Woodcraft.* It deals with the immediate post-Revolutionary period and the efforts of Captain Porgy to reestablish his ravished plantation on the Ashepoo. Though there are moments of exciting action in it, the novel is virtually a study of social issues raised during the Revolution but not resolved by it. This work, the most popular of the Revolutionary romances with present-day readers, is peculiarly interesting in that it is a kind of nineteenth-century *Soldier's Pay* and a picture of Snopesism beginning to raise its head, as the lowest level of society begins to influence the political and economic life of the region. These two novels form a third group, one concerned essentially with social and political issues rather than with questions of military action and strategy.

A fourth group is formed by *The Forayers* (1855) and its sequel *Eutaw* (1856), really one continuous novel of 1,142 pages. Simms in this long narrative returned to the civil strife during the closing months of the Revolution in South Carolina and portrayed in great detail the relentless conflict of patriot families and soldiers against the marauding bands of loyalists, who were ravaging the countryside. Here he explored anew the bases upon which the Revolution was fought, and here he made his strongest argument about loyalism and patriotism in the state.

After *Eutaw* he published only one other book-length novel, *The Cassique of Kiawah* (1859), a romance of the seventeenth-century colony. He returned once more to the Revolutionary War in fiction, in 1867, when he published *Joscelyn: A Tale of the Revolution* serially in the *Old Guard Magazine*.[19] The story is laid around Augusta, Georgia, and in Up Country South Carolina in the opening days of the conflict, when friend is taking side against friend, and loyalist and rebel are struggling to define their roles. But now the sympathy and understanding for the loyalists that he had once shown have faded. *Joscelyn* is incomplete, ending in a way not uncommon in Simms's career, as the characters are still caught up in an unresolved plot and their fate and fortunes remain, he says, to be spoken of in future pages. Those pages were never written, and *Joscelyn* did not find its way between book covers until its publication in the Centennial Edition of The Writings of William Gilmore Simms in 1975.[20] Its primary value to the study of Simms and the Revolution is that it shows how dark and embittered he had grown by 1867.

The concept of revolution and the role of the Revolutionary War in the history of America were topics which had interested Simms throughout his career. This career covered a period that contained two major revolutionary movements in Europe—the Revolution of 1830 in France, which led Simms to write a long poem entitled *The Tri-Color, or the Three Days of Blood, in Paris*[21]—and the

Revolutions of 1848, which seemed to a conservative southerner to threaten the stability of the world. Newspapers published in South Carolina between 1830 and 1850 show the degree to which the events of Europe in turmoil and revolution attracted the attention of the editors and, one would presume, of their readers.

The American Revolution was for Simms not merely annals in the epical record of a heroic people's resistance to tyranny and struggle for freedom; it was also the principal historical event in the life of the nation. In a series of lectures Simms delivered in 1842 on "The Epochs and Events of American History, as Suited to the Purposes of Art in Fiction" he seeks in American history for events appropriate to representation in fiction. These lectures show that among such events were those of the Revolution, where he could depend upon oral traditions at the same time that he could display the conflict of the old and the new, the struggle between an old age passing and a new age struggling to be born, a situation which is at the heart of the novels of Sir Walter Scott, whom Simms regarded as his great literary master.[22]

Furthermore, from 1828 on, the state of South Carolina had been in conflict with certain policies of the federal government—over tariff, over slavery, over outside interference, and over representation.[23] In addition, the growing abolition movement placed the South and its peculiar institution under increasingly angry and intemperate attack. Among the many things which were difficult to accept without making bitter responses were statements such as John Greenleaf Whittier's poem "Massachusetts to Virginia":

What means the Old Dominion? Hath she forgot the day
When o'er her conquered valleys swept the Briton's
  steel array?
How, side by side with sons of hers, the Massachusetts men
Encountered Tarleton's charge of fire, and stout
  Cornwallis, then?

Forgets she how the Bay State, in answer to the call
Of her old Houses of Burgesses, spoke from Faneuil
   Hall?
When, echoing back her Henry's cry, came pulsing on
   each breath
Of Northern winds the thrilling sounds of "Liberty
   or Death!"

What asks the Old Dominion? If now her sons have
   proved
False to their fathers' memory, false to the faith
   they loved;
If she can scoff at Freedom, and its great charter
   spurn,
Must we of Massachusetts from truth and duty turn?[24]

In 1847 Lorenzo Sabine published a pioneering historical work, *The American Loyalist, or Biographical Sketches of Adherents to The British Crown in the War of the Revolution,* in which he condemned South Carolina for making virtually no contribution to the cause of American freedom. He said:

> She did not [contribute to the regular army one-half as many soldiers as New Hampshire]; she could not defend herself against her own Tories; and it is hardly an exaggeration to add, that more Whigs of New England were sent to her aid, and now lie buried in her soil, than she sent from it to every scene of strife from Lexington to Yorktown. . . . It was a hard duty to determine . . . which party [in South Carolina] was guilty of the greatest barbarities. . . . Whatever the guilt of the Tories, the Whigs disgraced their cause and the American name.[25]

Simms's reaction to Sabine's work was quick and indignant. He wrote periodical essays,[26] which were later published as a volume entitled *South Carolina in the Revolutionary War: Being a Reply to Certain Misrepresentations and Mistakes of Recent Writers, in Relation to the Course and Conduct of This State,*[27] in which he attacked Sabine's facts and rejected his conclusions. He began to find in works like John Pendleton Kennedy's *Horse-Shoe Robinson,* an historical novel of the Tory ascendancy in South

Carolina, which he had admired in 1835, much to refute in 1852 when he wrote a long review of the revised edition.[28] Although there are parts of his own novels, *The Partisan, Mellichampe,* and *The Scout,* which could have been used to illustrate at least a portion of what Sabine said in *The American Loyalist* and which stated attitudes toward the Tories similar to Kennedy's in *Horse-Shoe Robinson,* Simms's view of the loyalists and of South Carolina's participation in the Revolution underwent serious modification. By 1850 it was necessary to defend the state against the charge of having failed to do its duty in the fight for national independence.

During the 1840s Simms was extremely active in the Young America Movement, and he declared accurately in 1842, "I am an ultra-American, a born Southron, and a resolute loco-foco."[29] He participated actively in the campaign for a national literature, and in 1845 he made the *Southern and Western Magazine,* popularly known as *Simms's Magazine,* virtually the southern voice of that basically New York group.[30] In 1847 he split with Young America over the presidential election, in which he supported Zachary Taylor because Taylor was a southerner and a slaveowner, but after Taylor had won the election, Simms was bitterly disappointed in Taylor's conduct. Out of these activities emerged strong reasons for Simms's need to defend his people against attacks from the outside, while there was within him a sense that many of the virtues of the past had been lost.[31] John Erskine in 1910 was correct in saying, "From the beginning to the end of his work he dwelt lovingly upon his country's past, with a sad sense of faded glory. The young Southerner now thinks of the days before the war as the happy prime of his state, and is melancholy over her lost battle-fields, but in that very prime Simms was thinking as sadly of the bright days of Revolutionary honor."[32] And in the novels he wrote about the Revolution after 1848, he seemed almost to be inviting the southern reader to ask himself whether the South had not exchanged the oppression of British rule for a greater despotism of federal mob rule.

The difficulty, of course, was with the issue of what the Revolution had been fought for. In the early novels there is little question that Simms saw it as a crusade waged to win freedom and justice for all. In *The Partisan* and *Mellichampe* and, to an appreciable extent, in *The Scout*, the concept of the Revolution as the opening act in the founding of a nation of justice against the oppression of a foreign power is clearly expressed; but beginning with *Katharine Walton* (1851), the Revolution became for Simms not so much a symbol of resistance to tyranny against the individual as the preservation of an endangered social order.

The Revolution in South Carolina was certainly very different in class structure and the nature of warfare from that in New England and the Middle Atlantic states. In the South the Revolution was virtually a civil war between patriot and loyalist, occurring concurrently with a series of formal military engagements. The war was actually won in South Carolina largely by the partisan warriors, guerilla fighters, under men like Sumter and Marion, who raided British outposts, attacked scouting parties, and played havoc with British lines of communication and supply. Certainly the final victory was shaped by Greene's Fabian tactics, but in large measure the campaign consisted of hundreds of minor engagements, most often between patriot and loyalist bands.[33]

The division of patriot and loyalist in the state was very sharp. Among the leading families hardly one was not split over the issue of their stand toward American independence.[34] In the lower orders of society were many discordant elements, and a pronounced sectional division also existed in the state. South of the fall line, a line running parallel to the coast and passing through the present city of Columbia, was the Low Country dominated by slaveowning, aristocratic planters and great merchants. North and west of this line were the thinly settled frontier communities populated by Scotch-Irish, Scotch, and Germans, most of whom had recently come down the old cattle trails from Pennsylvania and western Virginia. Between these two groups existed an animosity that has continued to the present day.[35] Because the war was generally considered to be aimed at benefiting the merchant and planter classes of Charleston and the Low Country, those of the Up Country instinctively disapproved of it.[36]

In May 1780, General Lincoln, the American defender of Charleston, surrendered his army to the British. The fall of Charleston meant the end of organized resistance in the colony, and Sir Henry Clinton reported, "There are few free men in South Carolina who are not either our prisoners or in arms with us."[37] Most of the leaders of the state militia—the predominant organized military force in South Carolina throughout the Revolutionary War—took protection from the British or fled, and the British maintained relatively small formal military force in the state, leaving its control largely in the hands of the American loyalists. George Bancroft said, "The property of the greatest part of the inhabitants of South Carolina was confiscated. Families were divided; patriots outlawed and savagely assassinated; houses burned; and women and children driven shelterless into the forest; districts so desolated that they seemed the abode only of orphans and widows."[38]

Clinton, on June 3, issued an order requiring all South Carolinians who had taken protection or parole from the British to bear arms for the British cause. This order made continued neutrality an impossibility, and every former American soldier still in the colony had to choose a side, no matter how often he found it expedient to change to another. The lowest classes seemed to have chosen sides for the Crown, either for the loot that might be gained or for revenge for the injuries they had sustained from the other side.[39]

Partisan bands under Williams, Sumter, Marion, and Pickens sprang up to harass the British in endless sudden forays and to exact a bloody vengeance from the equally merciless Tories. As John C. Miller says, "The British could not prevent the state from being drenched in blood. Tories and patriots were so evenly divided in the Carolinas and Georgia that this civil war was not, as in New England, a mere matter of mobs hounding a few outnumbered Tories, but war without quarter in which both sides committed gruesome atrocities."[40] Simms believed that most, though by no means all, of the patriots supported the established order and that those who supported the British were predominantly those trying to disrupt the order, by turning the social, economic, and political structure upside down, to gain for themselves special privileges they had not previously had.

Hence Simms modified his concept of the true purposes of the Revolution from his early view that it was a struggle for individual freedom to the view in the 1850s that it was fought essentially in defense of an established order. The villains were always the British, who in both views acted as despots, but this despotism came increasingly in Simms's mind to be exercised against social orders rather than individuals. Thus to lay the facts of the Revolution imaginatively before the people was, as he came to see it, to show that his beloved state had bravely, while standing virtually alone, resisted outside tyranny which struck at its central order. Simms obviously felt the parallel between that view of the Revolution and the situation that South Carolina found itself in in the 1840s and 1850s was instructive to South Carolina citizens. William R. Taylor has seen the growing interest of South Carolinians in the Revolution during this period as, in part, their adjustment to the feeling that it was necessary "to cut themselves off from the threatening implications of contemporary social ideals and moral values," and he adds, "Nowhere is this retreat more apparent than in the writings which attempted to find in the American Revolution a larger meaning for the South."[41] Thus Simms, the leading literary spokesman of his region, used the historical novel as a means of showing in the Revolution a usable past and one that would both justify the past actions of his state and rally its present inhabitants to the defense of their embattled traditions and institution.

To accomplish this goal in the treatment of a specific event in the history of his people, Simms had the example of the historical novels of Sir Walter Scott, in which Scott sought to dramatize climactic moments of conflict in history. Scott, in the prefaces to the Waverley Novels, is explicit about how he chose his periods and worked them up. He always selected a period for qualities associated with his concept of history and his concept of history, as Georg Lukács has pointed out,[42] is essentially that of Hegel. Scott sought an age of great contrast "in which the ancient and rough manners of a barbarous age are just becoming innovated upon and contrasted by the illumination of renewed or reformed religion."[43] The Revolution, when viewed as a primarily civil war between patriot and Tory,[44] certainly represented such a conflict and was one of the great historical moments when people were undergoing profound changes. The old colonial order was being destroyed and in its place a new state was being created. The figures in Simms's novels who embody the World-Historical Individual are the leaders of the partisan forces, men such as Marion and Sumter. In the Revolutionary romances Marion is the dominant figure that ties together not only the historical action but most of the personages in the separate plots. In the loving attention which Scott lavished upon the simple people and the low life of Scotland, there was ample illustration for Simms for the treatment of the mass of people who fought the almost nameless battles in unmarked places and by their small and nearly forgotten deeds shaped the course of a nation and turned the course of an empire. Hence Simms found in the Scott novels a form within which he could formulate a statement about the meaning of history and find in the past instructive moral lessons for the present.

In constructing his seven loosely linked novels about this period in American history Simms allowed the broad outline of the stories to be formed by the pattern of military events. The heart of British control in South Carolina was Charleston, which was protected by two rings of fortresses. An outer ring swept in a great arc from Augusta, Georgia, to Ninety-Six, to Camden, to Georgetown. An inner ring was formed by Granby (now Columbia), Orangeburg, Fort Motte, and Fort Watson. The plan of the Continental Army was not to win battles but to force the British army to withdraw from these fortresses into Charleston, thus freeing the state from military rule. Greene lost to Rawdon at Hobkirk's Hill outside Camden but so depleted the British forces that Rawdon was forced to abandon the city. Greene laid siege to Fort Ninety-Six, and although Rawdon rescued its garrison, the British lacked the troops to continue to man it, abandoned the fortress, and made a forced march to Orangeburg. The Americans and British fought a major battle at Eutaw Springs, where the British finally held the field but again at too high a price, and they were forced to withdraw into Charleston. At the time of Cornwallis's surrender at Yorktown, the British forces in South Carolina were bottled up in Charleston. Throughout these formal military movements the civil war between patriot and Tory went on with undiminished ferocity, and as British control slowly withdrew into Charleston, the dormant feud between Tory and patriot flared up in unrestrained butchery and robbery. Outlaws banded under desperados raided Whig and Tory alike. When the British evacuated Charleston in December of 1782, they left a state in which, according to Edward McCrady's count, 117 battles, actions, and engagements, most of them civilian and most of them minor, had taken place.[45] It was this essentially domestic conflict which Simms illustrated in his novels and from which he drew his lessons.

The first three of Simms's Revolutionary romances—*The Partisan, Mellichampe,* and *The Scout*—were constructed around what were even then highly conventional plots dealing with upper-class young lovers caught in conflicting ideological claims and the danger of war, but their true centers of interest were portrayals of common people and the low life which formed the backdrop against which these central plots took place. These common people are deeply engaged in the basic patriot-Tory conflict, and Simms in these first three novels portrays the horrors of that conflict with Gothic intensity and a strong sense of its mingled motives. There is no question of the side Simms has chosen in the struggle, but he does clearly recognize that the loyalists had a cause and that Whig fanaticism and brutality had made important contributions to the stand taken by many loyalists.[46] It was, he believed, the planter and the merchant classes who were the chief rebels against British rule, and it was the dispossessed and the downtrodden, those whom today we would call the poor whites, who principally rallied to the British, as much in opposition to their oppressors as in support of principle. In his *History of South Carolina* Simms wrote, "The common appeal of the loyalist leaders was to the vulgar prejudice against rank and wealth, the haughty assumptions of the citizens and planters of the seaboard and their free expenditure of the public money."[47] A goodly portion of his energies in these first three Revolutionary novels went into presenting the horrible and merciless aspect of the struggle. In *The Scout* he said,

We shall be compelled to display, along with its [partisan warfare's] virtues of courage, patriotism, and endurance, some of its crimes and horrors! ... South Carolina, at the period of our narrative, presented the terrible spectacle of an entire people in arms, and hourly engaging in the most sanguinary conflicts. The district of country called "Ninety-Six" ... is estimated to have had within its borders, at the close of the Revolution, no less than fifteen hundred widows and orphans, made so during its progress. Despair seems to have blinded the one party as effectually to the atrocity of their deeds, as that drunkenness of heart, which follows upon long-continued success, had made insensible the other.[48]

In the fourth of his Revolutionary romances, *Katharine Walton,* Simms moved to a different kind of story. There are still skirmishes and exciting battles in the swamps and countryside around Charleston, but the fundamental issues have to do not with military actions but with problems of loyalty, conduct, and honesty in the city of Charleston during the British occupation. The issues that really matter in this novel are fundamentally political. The question of the survival of the basically aristocratic order of the pre-Revolutionary colony is the central concern, and the issue of the British sequestration of patriot property serves as a symbol of tyranny and injustice from without. In many respects *Katharine Walton* is the most various and lively of Simms's Revolutionary novels, and it explores the problems of the choice of sides in the conflict and of loyalties to the sides chosen with great care and intensity. Plainly when he began writing this novel as a serial in 1849, his view of the basic issues of the Revolution had changed. *Katharine Walton* is ostensibly the conclusion to the story of Robert Singleton, which had been begun as the main plot in *The Partisan,* had continued as a subsidiary plot in *Mellichampe,* and reaches its happy conclusion with his marriage to Katharine Walton in this book. Simms had interrupted the trilogy to present a picture of the Revolution on the frontier in *The Scout,* the least representative of the Revolutionary romances. A tale of Gothic horrors, centered on a plot borrowed from Johann Friedrich von Schiller's *Die*

Räuber[49] and dealing with the siege of Fort Ninety-Six, it not only deals with the Up Country but also lacks the presence of General Francis Marion.

After *Katharine Walton*, Simms moved to the postwar period and portrayed in *Woodcraft* the rewards that the partisan warriors received at the end of the conflict: when the American armies marched triumphantly into Charleston, which the British had evacuated, the dirty and bedraggled partisan troops of General Marion were denied the right to march in the parade. The major comic character of the series and the protagonist of *Woodcraft* is Lieutenant and now Captain Porgy, a representation both of the virtues of intelligence, learning, and chivalry of the planter class and of its indolence, self-indulgence, and tendency to squander resources. Porgy has been a great and able soldier, and he is one of those who earned for the state the freedom from foreign tyranny it enjoys, but he comes home to find the land a prey to the lowest classes, to former loyalists, to squatters, and to poor whites. His own plantation has been stripped of its resources, and he must now start almost from the beginning and try by desperate hard work to win back that order and existence once represented by the ravaged plantation he had fought with valor, courage, and great daring to preserve during the long years of the war. Such an account would resound with themes familiar to the southerner who saw himself now as the oppressed victim of the nation the Revolution had created.

Simms has borrowed from his beloved Shakespeare the plot from *The Merry Wives of Windsor* and organized the novel around a comic story of Porgy's middle-aged and hapless love affairs, but *Woodcraft* is nonetheless the record of a man who has sacrificed for the total well-being only to find his sacrifice unrewarded by the order which succeeds the victory he has helped to win.

When he had completed this dark view of the end of the Revolution, Simms could have set aside the subject and turned to other themes, for he had made no pretense at any time to recounting the history of the Revolution in South Carolina from its beginning to its end. Yet he clearly felt in 1854, after he had revised for the Redfield Edition the earlier novels in the Revolutionary series, that there was something that he needed to say and that was as yet unsaid. So he set out to write a concluding volume which would center on the events leading up to and including the battle of Eutaw Springs, the final major engagement of the American and British forces in South Carolina before the British army's retreat into Charleston. What began as one book, to be entitled *Eutaw*, grew into two books, *The Forayers* and *Eutaw*, really one continuous novel despite their separate titles.[50] In them he examined the nature of the loyalist sympathizers and the Tory outlaw bands with a thoroughness that he had never used before. In the person of old Colonel Sinclair, an adherent to the British crown whose son, the protagonist of the novel, is an officer in Marion's army, he explores the problems of loyalty with a new thoroughness.

In *The Forayers* and *Eutaw* Simms himself believed he was extending somewhat "our usual province of His'l. Rom."[51] At first glance what he was doing that was new seems a little difficult to understand. There are numerous skirmishes and adventures of the standard sort and set-piece chapters in which battles are described in great detail, so all of this seems, at least on the surface, to be essentially the formula he had first used in 1835 with *The Partisan*, except that it is now done with a relaxed ease and assurance of touch the aspiring young novelist of 1835 had not yet acquired. He is also still using the central plot of star-crossed young lovers, in this case Willie Sinclair and Bertha Travis. However, the nature of their familial opposition has changed, for Sinclair's father is an aristocratic loyalist who is indignant at his son's being a rebel officer, and Bertha Travis's father is also a supporter of the Crown but of a much lower social order. The conflict of interests that separates the lovers is class rather than politics, and only when old Sinclair sees that the British are not supporting his class but giving aid to hoodlums and riff-raff is he willing to approve his son's patriot actions.

Simms had always thought of the historical novel as a teacher of moral lessons and an instructor of the present through the instrument of the past, and it is in the lesson that is here being given that *The Forayers* and *Eutaw* differ most significantly from what has gone before. One feels a reasonable degree of certainty that in reading over the five Revolutionary romances which he revised for the Redfield Edition Simms became aware of the fact that the social nature of the conflict which the Revolution represented in South Carolina and the extent to which it preserved the social order had not been made clear enough in what had gone before. Hence he creates in these novels a large panel within which he can portray the true nature of that conflict.

There exists here a rich and variegated crew of prime rascals, ruffians, and outcasts, vividly drawn, sharply characterized, and given racy and convincing idiom to speak. One of his greatest character creations is the desperate and vicious outlaw Joel Andrews, known to his band of ruffians as Hell-Fire Dick and Devil Dick. A deserter from the loyalist forces, the head of a gang of outlaws who are raiding the countryside, a man with a passion for Jamaica rum and playing cards and an abiding hatred for what he calls the "harrystocrats," Hell-Fire Dick has physical courage that is enormous, prodigious strength, and loyalty to no one. Murder and robbery have been his business for years, and there is no soft spot in him. He is possessed of enormous vitality and tremendous energy and conviction, and he is but one of a host of figures who crowd the pages of this book.

Among the qualities which make this crew of vicious

animals into Simms's most interesting and lively fictional portraits are the vigor and comic zest with which he portrays them, the delight he takes in their dialect, and his absolute certainty about their being criminally wrong, a certainty which keeps us from extending sympathy to them. These desperados are people of enormous energy who do terrible things with relish and gusto and who also suffer ghastly fates but fates they richly deserve. Simms's attitude toward them is not unlike that of the teller of a folk tall tale toward the viciousness and suffering in that tale, particularly the viciousness and suffering of the wicked and depraved or of the lower classes. Simms's auctorial tone is one of detachment, the civilized outsider's view, such as Joseph Glover Baldwin's in *Flush Times* or Augustus Baldwin Longstreet's in *Georgia Scenes* or George Washington Harris's in *Sut Lovingood Yarns*. This comic distance makes almost unspeakable horrors committed by the rascals and villains who populate the pages of these books palatable to the reader.

Simms traveled on horseback in 1847 in the mountains of western North Carolina, and there in hunting camps he had encountered the folk tale tradition which he embraced, which from this point on he used with some skill and distinction, and which gave him the means by which he was able to portray the full depravity of the loyalist side without producing the chilly horror of a Gothic tale.[52] It was a major artistic accomplishment; it lifted these last two full-length Revolutionary romances onto a different level from those that had gone before and made them, though clearly too long and too confused in central plot, the finest writing Simms did anywhere.

In them he was able to assert, in persuasive fictional form, the claim that he had been making in addresses and in articles since the late 1840s—that the Revolution in the South was won by the partisan soldier and that South Carolina had done more than its share in winning the nation's independence. These novels assert, through illustrative episode, that everywhere that the Continental Army fought—at Hobkirk's Hill, at Fort Ninety-Six, at Orangeburg, at Eutaw Springs—it was defeated and that the series of victories which truly precipitated the end of the Revolution in South Carolina and forced the British armies toward surrender at Yorktown was constructed by the South Carolina militia men who conquered the small garrisons and outposts of the British and made their longer possession of the land impossible. The victory rested, Simms asserts, on skirmishes in almost nameless places like Fort Motte, Fort Watson, Fort Granby, Georgetown, Augusta, Silver Bluff, Biggins Church, Dorchester. It was not that Simms did not admire General Greene, whose biography he had written, but that he wanted to emphasize the extent to which Greene's successful Fabian strategy depended upon efforts of the partisan troops. To indicate this position most emphatically a significant shift had to occur in Simms's purposes and in the emphasis that he placed on historical treatment in *The Forayers* and *Eutaw*. The result is that, trite though their form seems to be, these two Revolutionary romances do indeed break new ground for Simms in his interpretation of the nature of the Revolutionary struggle.

William Gilmore Simms, in creating his ambitious panel of novels dealing with the American Revolution, was thoroughly attuned to the South, whose literary spokesman he aspired to be and clearly became. From 1835 to 1856, he saw the American Revolution in terms of the historical process of which it was a part. He attempted to preserve about it the memories and traditions which were known to him and dear to him, and, putting together memory, tradition, formal history, and romance of the type of the novels of Sir Walter Scott, he tried to say to his contemporary readers what the past meant and how it should be applied. As his view of the position of his state and his region changed between 1835 and 1856 the way in which he interpreted the Revolution also changed, but the essential nature of the meaning of history, the sense that we learn fruitful and truthful lessons from the past through what happens in time rather than space, that history indeed is one vast instructive process by which opposing positions somehow find a synthesis and, above all, that in the pictures of the past we can read instructive lessons for the future were positions which he never deserted.

As we look back upon his work and realize that in large measure his use of the American Revolution was a political use, made in support of a regional position and in defense of the institution of slavery, we can understand why critics and literary historians find it hard to take his Revolutionary romances with the utmost seriousness. Yet, we must acknowledge that, given his postulates about the nature and the meaning of history and given the strong presupposition of most southerners that the social structure is more important than the individual, we can understand what he did and see that perhaps more clearly in Simms's seven linked Revolutionary romances than in any other work of fiction done before the Civil War the South found an epic statement of its ideals and its purposes and a gallant defense of the role it had played in the making of the nation.

Simms was but one of many southern novelists who used and still continue to use the Scott model for the representation of crucial events in the historical past, usually about the Revolution and the Civil War. By the time of the Civil War, the form no longer proved challenging to the most ambitious novelists, but it continued to be effective for the representation of its limited view of the historical past.

The best antebellum southern novelists used it as a still challenging genre: John Pendleton Kennedy, in *Horse-Shoe Robinson* (1835) portrayed the period of the Tory triumph in the Carolinas, culminating in a justly famous description of the Battle of Kings Mountain, and in *Rob of the Bowl* (1838) drew a picture of colonial Maryland that owed as much to Thackeray as it did to Scott. William Alexander Caruthers laid *The Cavaliers of Virginia* (1835) during Bacon's Rebellion and *The Knights of the Horse Shoe* (1845) around Governor Spotswood's expedition to the Blue Ridge Mountains. John Esten Cooke, after Simms the most prolific of the nineteenth-century southern novelists, before the Civil War wrote several romances of colonial Virginia, the best being *Leather Stocking and Silk* (1852), *The Virginia Comedians* (1854), and *Henry St. John, Gentleman* (1859). In his Civil War novels, *Surry of Eagle's-Nest* (1866), *Mohun* (1869), and *Hilt to Hilt* (1869), although he was writing from personal experience, he followed Simms in using the Revolution as a symbol of the South's struggle for freedom.[53]

After the Civil War, the best novelistic talent was attracted to local color and realism, but writers of talent still turned to the historical novel for the representation of the past, as Mary Johnston did for her long series of Virginia historical romances. James Boyd in *Drums* (1926), set in Revolutionary Carolina, *Marching On* (1927), laid during the Civil War, and *Long Hunt* (1930), a frontier novel, worked in the Scott tradition with considerable success. In 1975 the Pulitzer Prize for Fiction was given to Michael Shaara, a native of New Jersey who has lived in the South for the past two decades, for his moving and detailed account of the Battle of Gettysburg, *The Killer Angels: A Novel* (1974). This fine novel uses history and historical data directly, clearly, and accurately; it is a triumph of the use of the "classic" historical novel, and it shows the continued vitality of the form invented by Sir Walter Scott.

3
"Time . . . The Sheath Enfolding Experience": The Past as a Way of Life

> . . . what I say of Philadelphia *now*
> Is true, but true now only, not true *then*.
> But this much then: We knew we were only men
> Caught in our errors and interests. But I, a man,
> Suddenly saw in every face, face after face,
> The bleared, the puffed, the lank, the lean, all,
> On all saw the brightness blaze, and I knew my own days,
> Times, hopes, books, horsemanship, the praise of peers,
> Delight, desire, and even my love, but straw
> Fit for the flame. . . .
> —Thomas Jefferson, in Robert Penn Warren's
> *Brother to Dragons*[1]

THE CIVIL WAR was the watershed in southern history. Before that cataclysm there had been an Old South that was aristocratic in aspiration, however much the work of its world was done by a yeoman citizenry. It had rested upon ideals of grace, honor, dignity, chivalry, and violence, all made possible by chattel slavery. Southerners looking backward have tended to view that Old South as a kind of Eden and to see the Civil War as a bloody expulsion from that Eden. For the Civil War brought that Old South to an end and replaced it with a period of vast adjustment in which the class structure of the region underwent major transformation. The British soldiers at Yorktown marched to their surrender with the sounds in their ears of the band playing "The World Turned Upside Down"; had there been bands playing at Appomattox Court House the southerners there might well have heard the same derisive tune. In the aftermath of that war the South was an occupied territory being forcefully reconstructed, and the social classes that had for long been dominant were replaced through the rise to power of the middle and lower classes.

For those interested in history as process the sequence of Old South, Civil War, and Reconstruction forms a greatly accelerated instance of the classic historical novelist's ideal historical moment. It is as though one of Scott's crucial ages in history had been compressed into the period of a quarter of a century in which a civilization and culture had been defeated and violently displaced.

Despite the hundreds of novels about it, the Civil War has received little effective fictional treatment. In a study of American writers in the Civil War, Daniel Aaron found little of primary literary value and almost nothing in the Confederate South that attracted his attention.[2] John Esten Cooke's *Surry of Eagle's-Nest* (1866) and its sequel *Mohun* (1869), which cover the bulk of the battles of Lee's army, and *Hilt to Hilt* (1869), a story of Mosby's guerillas, are romances based upon the military action of the Civil War, but they are works of negligible value; Cooke's earlier novels of colonial Virginia and the Revolution remain his primary claims to fame. Sidney Lanier's *Tiger-Lilies* (1867) is a novel written out of personal experience, as Cooke's had been, but if we celebrate Lanier, we celebrate him for his poetry. It is perhaps true, as Aaron asserts, that the southern record of the Civil War is essentially the "unwritten novel" and that it can best be described in works such as Mrs. Mary Chestnut's diary.[3] Of the efforts to deal with the Civil War in military terms as a basis for fiction, the Virginian Mary Johnston's two very long and detailed novels *The Long Roll* (1911) and *Cease Firing* (1912) are perhaps the best examples. Her presentation of Confederate military operations both at the level of command and of the rear rank is justly famous.[4] Yet these novels remain essentially, as Louis Rubin has suggested, "fictionalized history, with characters designed primarily to furnish individual plot suspense and thus to give body to the historical events of the War."[5]

The Civil War has certainly not been ignored as a subject for fiction; there has been a virtual industry in the production of Civil War novels. Robert A. Lively, in 1957, in *Fiction Fights the Civil War*[6] examined more than 560 novels dealing with the war, and the production has not ceased, but the best southern novelists have in most cases used the Civil War only indirectly.

There may be various reasons for this failure, among them the fact that all civil wars are events of such peculiar intensity and bitterness that decades and even centuries pass before writers find themselves able to deal with them without unconscious flinching or sentimental shutting of the eyes. The English civil war, too, produced little major literary work.

It is the attempt to come to terms with their past that leads most southern novelists to deal with history. We might expect the southern novelist, being the inheritor of a war which was lost in support of a cause today considered morally reprehensible, to try to shut his eyes to that past and to its meaning and, by embracing a Nietzschean view of history, to attempt to confine his vision to his limited, present being in a subjective world where the shape of history is irrelevant. Such has not proved to be the case. The impact of defeat, suffering, and reconstruction upon the South has been profound. C. Vann Woodward has pointed out that "The South had undergone an experience that it could share with no other part of America—though it is shared by nearly all the peoples of Europe and Asia—the experience of military defeat, occupation, and reconstruction. Nothing about this history was conducive to the theory that the South was a darling of divine providence."[7] Arnold J. Toynbee recalls having felt in 1897 that "history is something unpleasant that happens to other people," and then having realized that had he been born in the southern part of the United States, "I should then have known from my parents that history has happened to my people in my part of the world."[8] To believe in the value of a community and that the individual finds a significant part of the meaning of his life through his role in that community, and to be confronted with the fact that the ideals of that community have suffered overwhelming defeat places one with a propensity toward the Hegelian view of time and history in a position where the past begins to haunt the imagination and where understanding what that past was becomes peculiarly essential.

This backward look to a better and different world was typical of the South from the earliest days of the republic, and it was intensified by the Civil War and the Reconstruction. Although the southern psyche flinched away from too close a staring at the deeds on literal battlefields, there developed a powerful impulse among southern writers to reconstruct and understand that lost world.

Thus the South's concern with history made the social changes produced by the Civil War an inevitable subject for extended fictional treatment, and some of the best novelists of the South turned their attention fruitfully to the examination of those events. In doing so, they fell into two distinct groups, and each group tended to develop a special form for dealing with this subject matter. One group has been interested primarily in the social change that occurred as a result of the Civil War, and it has produced a kind of historical novel much closer to the strict novel of manners than the traditional historical novel has been. The other group has tried to inquire into the nature of the past, how we can know it, and how we can deal with the guilt which it has created for us, and it has developed highly sophisticated novelistic techniques. I shall deal with the first group in this chapter and with the other in the succeeding chapter, but in both cases I shall be forced to deal in a highly selective and broadly generalized way, choosing three or four writers and a few books to illustrate what I believe to be broad tendencies in the southerner's attempt to come to terms with his past.

Some who wished to reconstruct this lost world gazed at it through an apologetic haze as Thomas Nelson Page did in *In Ole Virginia* (1887) and *Red Rock* (1898). Such celebrations of the past, viewed through an almost religious glow, became the stock in trade of many defensive southerners, who gave romantically sentimental presentations of a past society idealized almost beyond the point of credibility. Page himself described its quality and its unreality in the brief preface that he wrote for a beautifully illustrated edition of *The Old Gentleman of the Black Stock*, in which he says, "For the old section of that Ancient Town through which the Old Gentleman of the Black Stock moved gravely in the years when the lover-scarred Beech shaded his tangled yard, and which Elizabeth Dale lighted with her presence, has quite passed away. Cinderella's coach comes along only in the Fairy-time of Youth."[9] In the period between 1890 and 1910, when the historical novel flourished everywhere, the South seemed to be winning in the book stalls the war it had lost on the battlefield,[10] and Page's method predominated in attempts to reconstruct a South before and during the Civil War which partook, as Page said, "of the philosophical tone of the Grecian, of the dominant spirit of the Roman, and of the guardfulness of individual rights of the Saxon civilization. And over all brooded a softness and beauty, the joint product of Chivalry and Christianity."[11]

Other southerners reconstructed the past angrily, with the venom of hatred and bitterness, such as Thomas Dixon, Jr., in *The Leopard's Spots* (1902) and *The Clansman* (1905), where the record is shaped to the pattern of his own passionately held political and social beliefs and presented in anger and dark despair.[12]

The form most attractive to those concerned with the serious fictional reexamination and recreation of the southern past was the novel of manners, a form of the novel which attempts to define the character and quality of a culture or a class in a particular time and place rather than to give its primary emphasis to individuals within that class. It is concerned with the patterns of conduct, codes of honor, communally shared beliefs about morality, ethics, and behavior, and agreed-upon ceremonies and rituals which shape the external elements of a way of life. It usually deals with a society in which, as Edith Wharton once remarked, "The characters talk in hieroglyphics." The Old South, with its stable social structure, its hierarchy of classes, its famous code of honor, its love of gracious living, and its formal public rituals and ceremonies lends itself peculiarly effectively to the sort of representation usually found in the novels of manners. Perhaps only the Knickerbocker society of New York and the high society of Philadelphia have equalled or surpassed the Old South as a mode of life peculiarly suited to such representation. Yet in America the novel of manners has been only rarely practiced, and there are many who maintain that it is not possible for it to be used authentically. Many feel that the novel of manners, which describes the outer forms of a relatively closed society in which characters are tested against these forms as a relatively inflexible yardstick of conduct and belief, cannot exist in a nation with highly fluid classes where social change rather than social stability is the common characteristic.[13] But the American novelist of manners has always been concerned with the impact that democracy makes on manners, so that he tests characters not by established standards but by their reaction under the impact of change. Thus his subject becomes mutability rather than order, and his testing cruxes occur when change rather than stasis places stress on the moral values of his characters. The form which emerged from the efforts to reproduce the life of the Old South through the Civil War and into the Reconstruction utilized this peculiarly American kind of the novel of manners, for these novelists were dealing with not only fixed manners and social structure but also the cataclysm through which those fixed manners and that social structure underwent major change. In using the novel of manners as the tool for dealing with the past, the southern novelist was not departing in a major way from the classical historical mode, for Ernest A. Baker has argued that the Scott novel itself is essentially a novel of manners laid in the past.[14] But certainly the emphasis given to the elements in the historical novel underwent significant change in the hands of these practitioners.

In the new form that resulted, the southerner's persistent sense of community[15] and of the importance of the structure of society was brought into some kind of balance with the novelist's instinctive concern with people and the development and changes in individual character, which has its counterpart in the southerner's strong sense of independence and personal dignity. The result has been an enormously revivifying tension through an examination of the individual's beliefs, commitments, emotions, and ambitions against the pattern of the society about him. These novels have tended to present the striving of the self for definition and self-realization against the strong sense of order, tradition, decorum, dignity, and grace which has been for a century and a half a truly major element of the southern character. The young man who stands in Allen Tate's "Ode to the Confederate Dead," where

> Row after row in strict impunity
> The headstones yield their names to the element,

and who, trapped in the solipsism of his present unhappy world can suggest to himself:

Turn your eyes to the immoderate past,
Turn to the inscrutable infantry rising
Demons out of the earth—they will not last.
Stonewall, Stonewall, and the sunken fields of hemp,
Shiloh, Antietam, Malvern Hill, Bull Run.
Lost in that orient of the thick-and-fast
You will curse the setting sun,[16]

is attempting to bring to the self the dignity and strength of a public order which is far and lost. He defines the essential position in which the characters of many of these novels find themselves. This concern with the private self and the public structure of society, with the interaction of past and present, is the dominant subject of some of the best historical fiction that the South has produced in this century. More like Thackeray than Scott, it is rich in the evocation of the quality of a way of life, and it is interested to only a minor degree in the representation of literal historical figures or of actual historical events. I should like to look briefly at a few representative works by Ellen Glasgow, DuBose Heyward, Stark Young, Allen Tate, Margaret Mitchell, and Margaret Walker, all of whom are essentially historical novelists of manners.

In a long career that extended from 1897 to 1945, Ellen Glasgow produced nineteen novels, the overwhelming bulk of them being fictional studies in the social history of Virginia. Her best work has, she asserts, a place in a consciously calculated social history of Virginia,[17] which traces "The transition, from an aristocratic to a commercial civilization,"[18] and shows "the rise of the middle class as the dominant force in Southern democracy."[19] Her collection of critical essays, *A Certain Measure*, is in a sense a definition of the interlocking structure of thirteen of her novels into a coordinated history of the social changes which marked Virginia from the 1850s to 1942.[20] James Branch Cabell denies this theory and suggests that he proposed the notion of a coordinated social history to her long after many of the books had been written.[21] Critics have found themselves in varying positions on this issue,[22] but whether consciously designed as Ellen Glasgow suggests or belatedly recognized to have an historical unity, as Cabell says, the bulk of Ellen Glasgow's work does indeed form what she claims it to be, a social history.

The one of her books which contains the most strictly historical elements is *The Battle-Ground,* and I shall examine it in some detail for this reason and also because it adumbrates the development of the historical novel of manners in the South. It is the only one of her books whose action lies entirely outside her own life span and whose events had to be reconstructed from various sources without the benefit of memory, even dimly from early childhood. It encompasses the greatest crucial issue in southern history, the Civil War, and it brings its characters through the most complete historically necessitated reversal of fortune of any of her works. It is also her only war novel and her only direct portrayal of life in the antebellum South. Hence, it constitutes a very good example through which to look at her use of history in fiction.[23] For she saw history as something that could best be written "in the more freely interpretative form of fiction."[24] Out of what she called her "intimate feeling for the spirit of the past, and the lingering poetry of time and place,"[25] she fashioned novels that were forms of social history.

In the preface to the "Old Dominion Edition" of *The Battle-Ground* she tells us that in writing that novel she was acting on her belief that "it might be interesting to look beneath the costume into the character of a civilization."[26] Indeed what she is attempting in *The Battle-Ground* is no less than a full-scale portrayal of Virginia aristocratic life before and after it was sundered by the bloody knife of the Civil War.

A substantial amount of historical research went into

the making of the novel. From her childhood the Civil War had been one of the subjects which she had heard insistently from her mother, "supported by a chanting chorus of male and female voices."[27] Her mother had survived the war in the devastated Valley of Virginia with unaltered courage but permanently broken health. Her governess, Virginia Rawlings, had an endless flood of stories of the war.[28] Some of the characters in the book were drawn directly from life, but they were people whom she had not seen with the eyes of the flesh but had created with the eyes of the imagination out of the stories and legends of her family. Major Lightfoot was modeled on a kinsman of her father's who was an elderly statesman and a violent noncombatant. Mrs. Lightfoot was drawn from a great grand-aunt on her mother's side of the family.[29] Her great aunt Cassie had saved ancestral portraits from the burning of her home named "Mount Joy"[30]—the basis for the hero's name Montjoy in the novel. Ellen's mother had stories of extreme hardship which she had suffered in the war herself and expressed the grave misgivings about slavery which Governor Ambler utters in the novel.[31] This body of family tradition and portraiture is like that upon which William Gilmore Simms claimed to have based the bulk of his Revolutionary romances. Simms cited as a principal source for these romances, "that venerable and moss-mantled Druid, Tradition,"[32] and said that he had "had his lessons at the knees of those who were young spectators in the grand panorama of our Revolution . . . venerable friends and loving kinswomen."[33] It is also much like the family traditions which Quentin Compson uses to reproduce the history of the House of Sutpen in *Absalom, Absalom!* There is a pattern in the southern writer's dependence upon oral and familial tradition for his historical work.

She also used more traditional forms of research. While she was writing the book, she had the complete files from 1860 to 1865 of the Richmond *Enquirer*, the

Richmond *Examiner,* and the New York *Herald.*[34] She went to the Valley of Virginia and traveled over the physical settings of the novel while she outlined the story. She read, she said, "innumerable diaries and letters."[35] She and her sister Cary toured the battlefields by hired carriage.[36] All in all, *The Battle-Ground* rested upon a solid basis of historical record, journalistic account, family tradition, and personal experience. When thirty-eight years later she revised the book, she declared, "As a whole I could find no obvious error either of fact or of atmosphere.... I could detect no flaw in the verisimilitude of the picture."[37] But she was absorbing the impressions made by these materials rather than taking the painstakingly exact notes of a historian's research. What she wanted was the texture and feel of the life, and she said, "Always I was collecting impressions rather than facts."[38] The intention was not to make a tale of historical incidents or to render precise accounts of military movements and battles; it was, as she said, to create an "evocation of a lost way of living."[39]

The Battle-Ground is truly a novel of manners laid in the past with a great emphasis on a way of life, on customs, mores, conventions, ideals, qualities of dress and speech, and ritual social ceremonies. It communicates a feeling in its first two books very much like that of James Fenimore Cooper's *The Pioneers.* Both books center on traditional communal ceremonies, including a Christmas celebration, and through those ceremonies, the authors lay before the readers the quality of the life of the people at the time of action of the story and reveal the essence of a special culture—in Cooper's case the settler's world on the banks of Lake Otsego in the 1790s, in Ellen Glasgow's, the aristocratic Virginia culture in the 1850s.

Then the Civil War violently interrupts this way of life and converts the nature of the culture by the eruption of sudden new forces. While she was writing the novel, Ellen Glasgow said in a letter to Walter Hines Page, "The usual war novel of our country is detestable to me—I want to do something different—to make, as it were, a picture of varied characters who lived and loved and suffered during those years and to show the effects of the times upon the development of their natures."[40]

"What I tried to do in *The Battle-Ground*," she later said, "was to write, not literally a novel of war, but a chronicle of two neighbouring families, the Amblers and the Lightfoots, who had lived through a disastrous period in history."[41] The story revolves around Betty Ambler, a redheaded, somewhat hoydenish girl, and Dandridge Montjoy, the grandson of Major Lightfoot. Montjoy is the son of Jane Lightfoot, who had eloped with a handsome, violent man and had been disinherited by her father. Upon her death, the boy comes to his grandfather's home, "Chericoke." The first half of the novel deals with the Lightfoots and the Amblers before the outbreak of the war. The second half follows Dan Montjoy, a volunteer in the Confederate Army, from the opening of the conflict to his return to a devastated home and the difficult task of constructing a new life for himself, Betty Ambler, and the other survivors.

She used the military history of the Civil War as a frame for the action of the second half of *The Battle-Ground,* following Dan Montjoy from the battle of First Manassas to Appomattox. But Ellen Glasgow simply assumes that the reader knows the military history and the geography of Virginia and that he will be able to identify actions as much as they need to be identified to understand the story. Indeed, to follow with any clarity the march of military events in the book it is necessary for the reader to impose upon the action of the story some of the structure of formal military history which Miss Glasgow's method prevents her giving. The battle of First Manassas and the forced winter march to Romney, Dan Montjoy's initiation into the realities of war, are told from the viewpoint of his own confused and bewildered impressions and have some of the characteristics of an impressionistic painting, which Stephen Crane's *The Red Badge of Courage* has. McClellan's advance on Richmond is told through the impressions of the civilian inhabitants of the city and is in no way a documented or detailed account of that event. What she declared to be her intention in the Old Dominion Edition preface seems to be quite accurate: "I attempted to treat the Civil War as one of several circumstances that molded not only the character of the individual Virginian but the social order in which he made a vital, if obscure, figure.... What interested me, however, was not so much the historical incidents (though I was careful to verify these to the smallest particular) as the deeper effects of that desperate, if fantastic, struggle upon the character of a civilization."[42]

Thus *The Battle-Ground* is in a sense a microcosm of the whole pattern of Ellen Glasgow's social history of Virginia. It opens with a long, loving, respectful, and yet gently and ironically amused picture of the Ambler and Lightfoot families as representative of the aristocratic culture which certainly did not numerically dominate antebellum Virginia but which did determine much of the pattern of antebellum Virginia life and shape the attitudes that led to its participation in the war. Almost exactly half of the story is devoted to describing the people who form the aristocratic and political leadership of the Commonwealth, to presenting their conflicts of attitudes toward secession (the Amblers are pro-Union, the Lightfoots pro-secession), to portraying the loyalty to Virginia which led people like Peyton Ambler, who hates slavery and disapproves of secession, to find himself in the front lines,[43] and to portraying the way in which young Virginians marched off to battle as though they were approaching a ball.[44]

The coming of the Civil War not only imperils the independence of the Commonwealth of Virginia, the power and control of the aristocracy which has governed its politics, and the security of the socioeconomic institution of slavery upon which that aristocracy quite clearly rested, it also introduced into the fabric of the Virginian's life a concept of democracy that differed significantly from the established aristocratic tradition. Ellen Glasgow said, "In *The Battle-Ground,* I have tried to portray the last stand in Virginia of the aristocratic tradition. . . . Any faith that molds and influences the plastic character of the people has validity for those who live under it and believe in it. The culture it creates and establishes is a reality so long as it survives." The first half of *The Battle-Ground* tries to establish that faith by a portrayal of those who hold it. Miss Glasgow said, "In the Old South, this inherited culture possessed grace and beauty and the inspiration of gaiety." And certainly her representation of the Amblers and the Lightfoots is in the best tradition of the novel of manners. It is in what happens to that culture when it is put to the test of war that we realize that, as she declared, "It was shallow-rooted at best, since, for all its charm and its good will, the way of living depended, not upon its own creative strength, but upon the enforced servitude of an alien race."[45]

She declared that nothing in her inquiries into the Civil War had interested her more than "the democratic feeling in the Army of Northern Virginia" where in the rank and file men who thought themselves to be aristocrats "marched on a level with men who did not care whether or not they were plebians." Her character Pinetop, a man who came down from his mountain cabin to follow Stonewall Jackson, a man "who had never owned a slave, and rarely seen one," was offering his life in defense, not of an abstract right, but of "institutions which bore more hardly upon the illiterate white man than they bore upon the black man in chattel slavery."[46] She was fascinated by instances in which men responded to the call of emotion and love of the land to perpetuate systems and institutions that worked to their own detriment. In the long episodes in the novel dealing with the friendship of the aristocrat Montjoy with the mountaineer Pinetop, she tried to define this democratizing effect of the Civil War.

This element in *The Battle-Ground* is effectively linked to a quiet but effective attack on slavery. When Montjoy discovers Pinetop trying to learn to read by piecing out letters with painful effort from a child's primer, he sees him for the first time as

> a victim to the timeless society in which he himself had moved—a society produced by that free labour which had degraded the white workman to the level of the serf.... Beside that genial plantation life which he had known he saw rising the wistful figure of the poor man doomed to conditions which he could not change.... In his [Montjoy's] sympathy for the slave, whose bondage he and his race had striven to make easy, he had overlooked the white sharer of the Negro's wrong. To men like Pinetop, slavery, stern or mild, could be but an equal menace, and yet these were the men who, when Virginia called, came from their little cabins in the mountains, who tied the flint-locks upon their muskets and fought uncomplainingly until the end. Not the need to protect a decaying institution, but the instinct in every free man to defend the soil, had brought Pinetop, as it had brought Dan, into the army of the South.[47]

Finally it all comes down to a bitter end in which little is left to the vanquished South except the stoic fortitude which ultimately becomes the supreme virtue in most of Ellen Glasgow's works. A defeated Montjoy, surveying the world that was left to him, meditates:

> So this was the end ... the end of his boyish ardour, his dream of fame upon the battle-field, his four years of daily sacrifice and suffering. This was the end of the flag for which he was ready to give his life three days ago. With his youth, his strength, his very bread thrown into the scale, he sat now with wrecked body and blighted mind, and saw his future turn to decay before his manhood was well begun. Where was the old buoyant spirit he had brought with him into the fight? Gone forever, and in its place he found his maimed and trembling hands, and limbs weakened by starvation as by long fever. His

virile youth was wasted in the slow struggle, his energy was sapped drop by drop; and at the last he saw himself burned out like the battle-fields, where the armies had closed and opened, leaving an impoverished and ruined soil. He had given himself for four years, and yet when the end came he had not earned so much as an empty title to take home for his reward.... Yes, this was the end, and he meant to face it standing with his back against the wall.[48]

Yet Dan knows that "despite the grim struggle and the wasted strength, despite the impoverished land and the nameless graves that filled it, despite even his own wrecked youth and the hard-fought fields where he had laid it down—despite all these a shadow was lifted from his people and it was worth the price."[49] And one realizes why it was that Ellen Glasgow declared that if she had lived before the Civil War she would have been an abolitionist.[50]

Before Dan Montjoy there stretches, therefore, a difficult world:

For a country that was not he had given himself as surely as the men who were buried where they fought, and his future would be but one long struggle to adjust himself to conditions in which he had no part. His proper nature was compacted of the old life which was gone forever—of its ease, of its gaiety, of its lavish pleasures. . . . now that it was swept away, he found himself like a man who stumbles on over the graves of his familiar friends. . . . the army was not the worst, he knew this now—the grapple with a courageous foe had served to quicken his pulses and nerve his hand—the worst was what came afterward, this sense of utter failure and the attempt to shape one's self to brutal necessity. In the future that opened before him he saw only a terrible patience which would perhaps grow into a second nature as the years went on.[51]

In a sense Ellen Glasgow has fashioned in this historical novel of manners, through the character of Dan Montjoy, a representation of the history of the Commonwealth of Virginia and the people whom she came from and whom she loved. Dan Montjoy unites the best of ease, grace, and gaiety with violence and dishonesty. He is thoroughly a part of the tradition of which he partakes through the generosity of his maternal grandfather, and yet the darkness that is in him through his paternal heritage makes him become a volunteer rather than an officer in the Army of Northern Virginia. His order exists upon the labor of slaves, about whom he feels responsibility and an unarticulated guilt. He takes arms to defend the soil he loves, fights through the bitter struggle, learns the value of a democratic society, is defeated in a conflict fought in part to preserve a dark institution of slavery, and at the end has stripped from him almost all the attributes of the graceful culture that he had had, and finally looks forward to a future that is drab and gray and that can be made into something livable only through the steady application of a stoic fortitude.

The battleground of the title of the novel is not solely the soil of Virginia. It is also the soul of the Virginia aristocrat, and on that battleground the Civil War almost became an objective symbol for an inner struggle which removed the ease, grace, and comfort of that life by taking from it the evil of slavery and that left it facing a rapidly changing world with only the courage and fortitude of its own gallantry to sustain it in the years to come. The rest of Ellen Glasgow's fictional history of Virginia was to trace the record of that fortitude and gallantry in the face of change. In her next novel *The Deliverance* (1904) she showed the terrible effects of this situation on Christopher Blake, a dispossessed aristocrat, and in *The Voice of The People* (1900) she had already shown the rise to power of the lower middle class. *The Battle-Ground* thus established the central social action that motivates her fictional history of the Commonwealth.

The long series of novels which follow portray in varying ways the methods by which the middle class accomplished its rise to the control of Virginia. In my opinion, a seriously neglected one of these is *The Romance of a Plain Man* (1909). In this novel Ben Starr, a poor boy rising through his efforts and looking with great longing upon the beautiful daughter of a formerly aristocratic family, succeeds in gaining great economic power, marries the girl, and in an effort to prove himself to her and to the world around him so commits himself to hard and endless work that he destroys the possibilities of a happy life. This book, not often discussed by Ellen Glasgow's critics, is a first-person narrative that succeeds remarkably well in persuading us of the reality of Ben Starr's climb to fame, of the motives which lead him to destroy his own happiness, and, as a picture of the newly arrived modern southern man frantically trying to reclaim the Old South virtues without understanding them, is a story with a poignant meaning.

Throughout her career Ellen Glasgow employed the novel of manners as a vehicle for discussing society, culture, and the community that she knew best. She found in it an effective form for what she wished to do, and she employed that form with true distinction through a long career in which she moved steadily to greater and greater accomplishments, a most unusual career for an American writer. Within her work is to be found one of the most telling records of the texture and quality of life in the Commonwealth of Virginia from the Civil War to the 1940s. Perhaps nowhere in America other than the South would anyone have undertaken such a task, and certainly nowhere else in America could that task have been handled with the seriousness and the success which Ellen Glasgow enjoyed over more than forty years. The southerner's obsession with the past, which can be haunting and destructive, in the hands of Ellen Glasgow was converted into an effective means of portraying a lost world and defining individuals in relation to it while certain statements of deep meaning are being made about the society in which we find ourselves.

Let us briefly glance at some of the other novelists who worked in this fruitful tradition.

In *Peter Ashley* (1932) DuBose Heyward presents a picture of life in Charleston on the eve of the Civil War so precise that it has been cited in at least one serious scholarly bibliography as a source for knowledge about William Gilmore Simms and his relation to Charleston and to Russell's Book Shop on the eve of the Civil War.[52] *Peter Ashley* is a lovingly drawn but by no means uncritical portrayal of life in the City by the Sea on the eve of the bloody conflict, and into this rich picture of the life of the city is introduced Peter Ashley, a young man educated in England, who must make, as many southerners in that time had to make, a choice between belief—in Ashley's case, a strong love for the Union and an active dislike of slavery—and the cause of the city-state of Charleston and the state of South Carolina. If the novel has a fundamental weakness, as I believe it does, it is that the dramatization of the inner life of Peter Ashley in conflict with the demands of the social order of which he is a part is only loosely related to the structure of the society which is being portrayed and to the events which mark the action of the book. *Peter Ashley* contains interesting accounts of military action in the Charleston harbor in the early days of the war, as those actions are viewed from the rooftops of Charleston's buildings by fascinated citizens, but its essential concern is with the quality of life in Charleston, the special strength of its appeal for Peter Ashley, and the decision he must make. Heyward achieves the by-no-means small accomplishment of making us feel at the end of the book, as Ashley goes off to war, that something approaching tragedy has taken place.

Stark Young's *So Red the Rose* (1934) is a lovingly detailed picture of life on two neighboring plantations in

Mississippi before, during, and just after the Civil War. Although lacking in formal plot, it is remarkably rich in evocative brief scenes. It alternates between Portobello, the home of the Bedfords, and Montrose, the home of the McGehees. There is division among the characters about the Union, about secession, and about slavery, but finally all of them come together in support of their gracious and civilized way of life, so that the novel becomes the portrait of a class just before and during the Civil War in and around the town of Natchez. The interrelationship of characters and the interweaving of events has a pattern that sometimes seems closer to the mingling of themes in a complex piece of music than it does to the normal structure of a novel. I have been assured by the historian Shelby Foote that *So Red the Rose* is historically accurate down to its smallest detail. However, though there are historical characters in the book and the action is shaped by events around Shiloh, the fall of Vicksburg, and Sherman's march through the South and although General Sherman is a major and fascinating actor in the novel, its final effect is almost that of a rich tapestry of manners with, appropriately for the novelist's obvious nostalgia, a sense of loss at what has passed away.

The looseness of structure allows Young the freedom to express directly what his story is intended to mean. He says, for example, of Charles Talliaferro, "He was a perfect example of a certain Southern type, planters' and lawyers' sons, who knew horses, rode well, hunted—were fine shots, had manners, a certain code of their own, and would not have been afraid of the devil himself."[53] Young sees the Old South as a highly admirable civilization and the New South which followed the surrender at Appomattox as a negation of that civilization and perhaps of all civilizations. Hugh McGehee brooding over the "new people" decides, "Where these people parted from him, where this new development left him, was the conception of life, the society, in which we are to lead our lives. . . . The truth was these people seemed to him to have no conception at all of a civilization."⁵⁴ Young, in *So Red the Rose,* is attempting to portray a meaningful past through picturing the order that was destroyed by the Civil War. Hugh McGehee seems to be speaking directly for his creator when he says, " 'The way I've been obliged to see it is this: our ideas and instincts work upon our memory of these people who have lived before us, and so they take on some clarity of outline. It's not to our credit to think we began today, and it's not to our glory to think we end today. All through time we keep coming in to the shore like waves—like waves.' "⁵⁵ *So Red the Rose* makes such an "outline" with consummate skill. It is an almost breathlessly beautiful reconstruction of a way of life, though as a novel the weakness of its plot line gives it difficulty in sustaining interest.

Margaret Mitchell's *Gone With the Wind* (1936), the most popular novel ever written by a southerner, is the best-known portrait ever drawn of the Old South, the Civil War, and Reconstruction. It differs from some of the other southern novels on these subjects in significant respects. One is the fact that it is set in middle Georgia and in Atlanta, a bustling new town and from even its prewar beginnings a symbol of the New South. Another is that its protagonists are disrespectful rebels against the order of the Old South. Scarlett O'Hara, the daughter of an Irishman who has married a southern aristocratic belle but is not himself in any sense an aristocrat, is the almost too obvious merging of the characteristics of her gracious mother Ellen and her bustling, "new man" father Gerald. Rhett Butler, the male protagonist, is the renegade son of Charleston aristocrats. As these two move through the coming of the war, the fall of Atlanta, the dangers of Reconstruction, and the rebuilding of Atlanta, they define largely through their active opposition the qualities of dignity, strength, and honor inherent in the old order and embodied, almost allegorically, in the figures of Melanie and Ashley Wilkes. Because the story of Scarlett O'Hara is an interesting tale and because Mrs. Mitchell has to a degree almost unsurpassed among American writers the storyteller's gift, her picture of southern life during the crucial period in its history has had wide acceptance. Yet Mrs. Mitchell goes on far beyond her need in setting down the details of actions, and she has an exasperating habit of playing a number of her big scenes off stage and then coming back to tell us the result.

The comparison of the southern historical novel of manners to Thackeray is perhaps nowhere more obvious than in *Gone With the Wind,* where most of the major characters have counterparts in *Vanity Fair* and many of the central situations also can be found in Thackeray's works. All in all the enthusiasm that developed for this huge novel—Ellen Glasgow liked it very much and Julia Peterkin praised it highly[56]—was probably well merited, although the success of the book in the marketplace has tended to create a not altogether justified skepticism among its critics. It is, for example, a far better story more effectively conducted than that in Stark Young's *So Red the Rose,* and it links the interior struggles of its characters with the exterior action of its events more effectively than DuBose Heyward did in *Peter Ashley.* The persistent although obvious irony resulting from telling the story from a narrative point of view inimical to the intent of the portrait removes much of the sentimentality that would have been present had the picture it paints of the Old South been drawn straight.

The southern historical novel which, I believe, must share with William Faulkner's *Absalom, Absalom!* the distinction of being the finest work of the southern historical imagination is Allen Tate's *The Fathers* (1938). In this novel Lacy Buchan is recalling from the vantage point of old age the experiences of his late adolescence in Virginia in 1860 and 1861. For Lacy the conflict between the private and the public life has been the essence of his being, and his narrative is a record of the complexity of that conflict. The protagonist of the story, George Posey, is defined against the life and traditions of the Old South. Posey himself represents the personal and private as opposed to the collective and public self, the modern as opposed to the old way of life. In a visionary moment Lacy sees that "The only expectancy that he [George Posey] shares with humanity is the pursuing grave, and the thought of extinction overwhelms him because he is entirely alone."[57] George is clearly a modern existential man, caught in the loneliness of his individual self, with the outside world lacking in meaning for him. This existential man is far from the typical man of the Old South. Lacy imagines that the ghost of his grandfather tells him, " 'My son, in my day we were never alone, as your brother-in-law [George Posey] is alone. He is alone like a tornado. His one purpose is to whirl and he brushes aside the obstacles in his way.' "[58]

Most of the novel, however, is concerned with the definition of the society within which George Posey lives without being a part and which is eradicated by the Civil War. George finally is a most effective device for delineating that society. Lacy says of it, "Our domestic manners and satisfactions were as impersonal as the United States Navy, and the belief widely held today, that man may live apart from the political order, that indeed the only humane and honorable satisfactions must be gained in spite of the public order, would have astounded most men of that time as a remote fantasy, impossible of realization."[59] Lacy, who functions as a witness with an extremely small role to play in the action, is learning about life from watching a series of catastrophes which present the meaning of life in an accelerated way. He says, "I witnessed an accumulation of disasters that brought about in our lives changes that would otherwise have taken two generations."[60]

The Fathers represents a peculiarly American form of a *Bildungsroman*, in which the young person learning how to live in a baffling and complex world acquires knowledge not through what he does or through what happens directly to him but by witnessing others in acts of conflict and meditating upon the meaning of their experiences.[61] Lacy Buchan has learned the dangers for a man of viewing himself as independent of society and its rules, by watching Posey—"a force that did not recognize the rules of his game"[62]—at a time when the old order had very sharply defined and precise rules, when it formed a community united by a code subscribed to by almost all those who were a part of it. This type of *Bildungsroman* has occurred many times in American fiction, but it has never been used more subtly or more effectively as a means of opposing an individual to society than in Tate's *The Fathers*, a truly brilliant novel of manners.

The structure of the book is of course shaped by the patterns of historical events, the battles, and the movements of troops in the early stages of the campaign in Virginia. But Lacy makes no effort to describe these events with any precision or exactness. Indeed he denies attempting to give his readers a sense of the pattern of these actions. At one point he says,

The day after secession a "body of troops," which swelled in the imagination of the people of our town into an "army," passed mysteriously through Manassas Junction; and in a few days we heard that the armory at Harper's Ferry had been captured. It was a great victory, of course, and Washington would be next. But what actually came next, what seemed so important at the time of its happening, I cannot remember, though I might consult the books and bring back the true order of events. It was at about this time, perhaps a little later, we heard that Massachusetts troops, marching through Baltimore, had been mobbed by the secessionists of Maryland.[63]

What Tate has accomplished in *The Fathers* is the creation of the quality and texture of a departed culture seen against the psychological needs, ambitions, and social and political desires of individuals living in this shaped and sharply disciplined world. One of the great weaknesses, it seems to me, of most of the criticism of Tate's novel has been to see it as a doctrinaire argument for a way of life. It is rather a complex, bewildering, and ambiguous picture of the interaction of individuals with a variety of contending ways of life, a prism that casts a different light with every new angle the reader assumes toward it.

Let me cite one other example of these novels of manners. Margaret Walker's *Jubilee* (1966) uses the materials that are common to the books we have been talking of—that is, the nature of the pre–Civil War culture in the South, the effect of that war, and the nature of Reconstruction—with the difference that in *Jubilee* these materials are treated from the viewpoint of the slave and the newly freed black man. A fictionalized biography of Miss Walker's grandmother, it is an intense and moving account of courage, endurance, survival, and love. But the qualities which give particular vigor to the novel result in substantial part from the tensions that develop in the characters through the conflicts between the hegemony of the slaveowners' culture, the so-called plantation tradition, and the hegemony which the slaves themselves created within that culture and attempted to sustain during the Civil War and into the Reconstruction. Miss Walker's novel describes the slave world as a subculture within that of the Old South and sees in it many characteristics that have been documented in great detail by the historian Eugene D. Genovese.[64] The publishers of the novel advertised it as a black *Gone With the Wind*, and in many respects the description is accurate, for the world of *Gone With the Wind* is reproduced here in elaborate detail and with qualities that are surprisingly like those defined in *The Battle-Ground, Gone With the Wind, The Fathers,* and *So Red the Rose,* but viewed from the underside of the society. Miss Walker, in constructing this novel out of the traditions and beliefs about her own family, is doing what southern novelists have consistently done in trying to describe this southern way of life around the Civil War—that is, to seek their own identity not through reaching within themselves for an interior self-expression but to seek that identity by looking back in time to the past and to the events which have made us what we are. Like all southerners Miss Walker, in looking back, sees clearly that the individual has a significant, indeed an imperative, relationship to the total culture of which he is a part.

Indeed all of these books remind us of what Margaret Mead once said, "Human cultures are the most distinctive creations of human beings, drawing as they do not only upon the special contributions of the singularly gifted, but upon the imagination, explicit and implicit, of every man, woman, and child who live within them, and through them, who, each generation, remodel the traditions which they have received from their cultural ancestors. But although human cultures are the most distinctive creations of the human, they are also the most fragile, for they live primarily in the habituated beings of living persons."[65] To find an adequate means to describe the aspects of a culture as fragile as this requires art more than science, and for the representation of such cultural phenomena the novel of manners is peculiarly well suited. Employing it in this way has given a new and different dimension to historical fiction. This dimension in the twentieth century has not been exclusively a southern property—for example, Willa Cather does something of the sort in her historical novels—but it has occurred in the South more frequently than anywhere else, and certainly it must be viewed as a product of a high esthetic and an artistic consciousness combined with the southerner's abiding sense of the indispensability of the essential but strangely irrecoverable past.

Each of the novelists we have examined has in differing ways set out to make what Ellen Glasgow declared her total work to be, a "chronicle of manners, which is integrated by the major theme of social transition."[66] Each has pursued his own artistic path and the technical differences among these novels is very great. But each, too, has imprisoned for us in the language of fiction an enduring sense of an evanescent period in time.

Certainly during the last forty years the realistic novel of manners has ceased to be such a primary challenge to the most talented and ambitious novelists, but the use of the methods of the realistic novel to convey a way of life has by no means ceased. Caroline Gordon, in *None Shall Look Back* (1937), a story of Bedford Forrest's Civil War campaigns, and *Green Centuries* (1941), a frontier novel, pursued this path with distinction. Gwen Bristow wrote a series of novels on the social history of Louisiana, and Lella Warren on Alabama, and they were simply two of many who drew detailed pictures of the life of past times. One of the most ambitious, at least in size, of these efforts to give substance to the life of past ages has been the series of eleven novels on colonial and Revolutionary North Carolina written by Inglis Fletcher between 1940 and 1962. Her motives, like those of Simms, are to portray the past through the reports of contemporaries and to show the extent to which the Revolution was a civil war, but she places great emphasis on the quality and texture of the life of the times and on the manners and customs. Her greatest weakness, aside from a pedestrian style, is her inability to fuse her central plots to the history she insists on recounting. She is properly discussed here to indicate a serious continuing interest in the life of the past and to show an indication of continuing popular interest in the historical novel of manners, for her novels sold very well. Jesse Hill Ford's *The Raider* (1976), a novel of the manners and life of west Tennessee before and during the Civil War, shows the continuing usefulness and vitality of the genre.

The southern novelist, during the ascendancy of realism as the dominant literary mode, found in the historical novel of manners an effective medium through which to pursue his interest in the past, and what he discovered is still useful and popular.

4
"To Grieve on Universal Bones": The Past as Burden

> ... your simpler world is ... always necessary—not a golden age, but the past imaginatively conceived and historically conceived in the strictest readings of the researchers. The past is always a rebuke to the present. ... It's a better rebuke than any dream of the future ... because historians will correct, and imagination will correct any notion of a simplistic ... golden age. The drama of the past that corrects us is the drama of our struggles to be human, or our struggles to define the values of our forebears in the face of their difficulties.
> —Robert Penn Warren, in *Fugitives' Reunion*[1]

ONE OF THE dominant characteristics of the southern mind is its concern with the past, with the events of history, and with the nature of society. In every period during the past one hundred and fifty years, southern writers have employed the currently popular literary forms to make their statements about the world and life, and important in those statements but differing in many instances from the rest of the nation has been their concern with their own history.

Before the Civil War, when the classical historical novel as conceived and raised to its height by Sir Walter Scott was the dominant literary form, southern novelists employed it, as did the rest of the nation, to create romance out of our immediate past. They found a fit subject for extended fiction in the clash of men, armies, and ideas in the American Revolutionary War. Thus when William Gilmore Simms wrote seven connected novels about the Revolution in South Carolina in an effort to describe that conflict, present its historical events and people, and defend the role of his state in it, he differed from other literary figures of his time only in continuing to use the historical novel as written by Scott after it had been abandoned as a literary model in the rest of the nation. We may condemn him for not making innovations in that form in the way, for example, that Nathaniel Hawthorne did in *The Scarlet Letter,* but we can hardly criticize him for using the historical novel as a form for the expression of his ideas.

When realism was the dominant literary form in America, the novel of manners was employed by the best of our southern novelists in an effort to describe and to define a society and to present the essential conflict in that society between the order and structure of the social world and the desire of the individual for freedom and the right to pursue his own dreams and ideals independent of the structure of the society of which he was a part. Whether the society thus described was romanticized or not, the works of people like Ellen Glasgow, DuBose Heyward, Stark Young, Margaret Mitchell, Allen Tate, and Margaret Walker were in keeping, in technique and method, with the challenging mode of realistic representation in their time. They employed these methods and techniques and the form of the novel of manners to describe the southern experience of the past, primarily from 1850 to 1900. As Arthur Mizener has said, in a fine study of Allen Tate's *The Fathers,* this is a novel thoroughly involved in the modern realistic tradition, and it succeeds in doing what Tate had set out to do, "to retain the great gains in sensuous immediacy won by the Jamesian or impressionist branch of the naturalistic tradition" and at the same time to employ "the realistic novel's image of life . . . the best means the novelist has for embodying that meaning and giving it life . . . the realistic novel's conventionalized representation of nature."[2]

During the last fifty years, novelists who had abandoned the historical form as a mode of serious expression also abandoned the realistic form as a primary mode of serious expression and turned toward representations of the world shaped more definitely by the author's point of view, his obsessions and commitments—that is, they turned away from realism back toward a new romanticism. As Arthur Mizener says, in a study generally inimical to the newer forms, the contemporary novelist seems to feel that "the representation of nature makes it impossible for him to express without falsification his strongest feelings" and thus he is willing "to sacrifice a probable presentation of the show of things to the direct expression of what the novelist thinks the things mean for the novelist."[3] This tendency has produced elaborate experimentation with form and technique, with dislocations in time, nonlogical narrative methods, and distortions in language in efforts to make statements of unarticulated feeling and to utilize improbability of action to describe a world of essentially allegorical meanings. The representation of a literal world, however complex, through the traditional modes of the novel of manners and the realistic tradition seems to most of these writers inadequate for the expression of what lies closest to their hearts and most deeply embedded in their souls.

Southerners have participated with remarkable success in this mode, and it was only a slight exaggeration when in 1959 Allen Tate said, "It is scarcely chauvinism on my part to point out that, with the exception of Fitzgerald and Hemingway, the region north of the Potomac and Ohio Rivers has become the step sister of American fiction."[4] Just before making this statement he had given a litany of southern writers, including Robert Penn Warren, Eudora Welty, Stark Young, Ellen Glasgow, James Branch Cabell, Katherine Anne Porter, Tennessee Williams, Thomas Wolfe, Caroline Gordon,

Flannery O'Connor, Ralph Ellison, John Crowe Ransom, and Donald Davidson. With few exceptions the names in such a list are names of writers who have experimented in various ways with the nature of narrative as the means of communicating a vision of the self and the world, and a goodly number of them have seen in history an appropriate and effective subject for their art, with the result that southern writers have been unusual in the nation during the past fifty years in turning talents of great ability to the exploration of the past and almost always doing it through experimental approaches to the art and craft of fiction.

The issues in which they are interested have been numerous and in a few instances reasonably traditional: the relation of the individual to his society, which had been so persistently the dominant theme of the realistic historical novels of manners; the question of whether we can know the past and of what history is and of how it functions, questions which raise profound epistemological issues; the question of whether a meaningful pattern exists in history, a question which begs itself, since no one uninterested in pattern in history ever asks the question; and a persistent effort to understand and expiate a collective and communal guilt which the region and its present denizens carry because of actions in the past. In almost all these cases the past rests heavily upon the serious southern novelist as a major burden to be borne and understood or as a collective guilt somehow to be recognized and expiated. At the heart of this burden of history has been the presence of the Negro and the shame of his enslavement and his second-class citizenship, the experience of military defeat, military occupation and reconstruction, and, largely as a result of this sequence of events, the presence through much of the region of a bone-gnawing poverty and hunger. This burden has created problems and raised tragic issues for the serious novelist. The strategies by which he has attempted to resolve those problems, or at least to state them clearly and honestly in the form of fiction, are varied, rewarding, and interesting. Let us look at a few examples. However, since almost all of these works have great complexity both on the level of surface expression and also of their deep structures, I must discuss them in terms of simple statements and generalized comments rather than in terms of any precise or exact analysis, as a result of the limitations of space.

Let us begin with Ellen Glasgow, who through most of her career functioned primarily as an ironic novelist of manners. In a book which she regarded as one of her two best, *The Sheltered Life*,[5] she interpolated a section of some forty pages in the middle of the story entitled "The Deep Past," a section that in terms of method is related closely to the "Time Passes" section from Virginia Woolf's *To the Lighthouse*, a book she greatly admired.[6] In "The Deep Past," which she called "the writing I should wish to be remembered by in the future,"[7] eighty-three-year-old General Archbald, sitting on a park bench in the sun, is contemplating the present action of the novel in terms of his own experiences in the deep past. He moves in recollection to a series of brief events out of his childhood and young manhood which enable him to understand the condition in which he sees the actors in the present drama being played in 1914 in Queenborough. As a child, desiring to be a poet and touched with a deep sense of pity for pain and suffering wherever he finds it and oppressed with the cruelty he sees everywhere in the world, he finds himself in the sharpest contrast to the essentially pitiless and violent order of the Old South. He recalls three principal events as he sits remembering. One is the experience of physical sickness when his grandfather, a great hunter, in disgust at his flinching from killing in the hunt, bloods him with the blood of a newly killed deer and calls him a milk sop when he vomits. Here he realizes that he cannot, as his mother had, accept "meekly, as an act of God's inscrutable wisdom, all the ancient wrongs and savage punishments of civilization."[8] The second episode occurs when, still a boy on the plantation, he helps an escaped slave to freedom by bringing him food, clothing, and a paper "ticket" taken from one of the slaves at his grandfather's home. Miss Glasgow says, "For the second time in his young life he was defying the established order, he was in conflict with the moral notions of men."[9] He had, she said, "taken his stand against the forces men about him called civilization."[10] The third event is a love affair he has in England with a married woman.

This dramatization within the wandering memory of an old man of experiences over half a century past defines how the triumph of society in the conflict of the individual with that society had to all practical purposes emasculated his moral courage and strength and left him weak and conforming, a supporter of the very order which had destroyed his possibilities for greatness. For General David Archbald had earned his title of "General" fighting in the Civil War, and later as an attorney he had become a stable pillar in the society against which he had revolted. Now at eighty-three, he can conclude calmly, "He had had a fair life. Nothing that he wanted, but everything that was good for him. He had been a good citizen, a successful lawyer, a faithful husband, an indulgent father; he had been, indeed, everything but himself. Always he had fallen into the right pattern; but the center of the pattern was missing."[11]

This section in *The Sheltered Life* defines the author's position, not only toward cruelty, pain, and suffering in the world—she was, like Thomas Hardy, whom she greatly admired, a vigorous crusader against cruelty to animals—it is also a comment on the nature of the society the Old South represented and in particular upon the debilitating effect that society had had with the passage of time on its best and most promising citizens. In order to make this statement, she has departed from her standard realistic method, which is employed with great skill through the bulk of the novel, and has moved into a kind of poetic recollection that moves freely in time, both borrowing sequential freedom from certain aspects of the stream of consciousness tradition and borrowing poetic expression from Virginia Woolf. The result is that "The Deep Past" is a narrative commentary upon the meaning of the rest of the story, a means by which Miss Glasgow tells us what the action of her novel represents as clearly as though she had interrupted the story for a while to talk in her own person.

There is almost no question that William Faulkner is a novelist strongly concerned with the past history of the southern region. The concept embodied in such a term as "The Yoknapatawpha Saga" rests on a sense of history and of time. Yoknapatawpha County, charted by Faulkner himself in a map in the first edition of *Absalom, Absalom!*[12] has a specific area and a specific population, but what is important about it is not the "postage stamp of earth" which it represents but the history, the classes, and the families which have existed upon that postage stamp of earth, from the days when it belonged to the Indians down to a time approaching the present in which Faulkner is writing.

In Faulkner's works we consistently understand, however hazily, the present in which we find ourselves by inquiring back into the pattern of events which created the present. This backward inquiry in time in Faulkner appears over and over again, perhaps nowhere more obviously than in the historical introductions to the sections of *Requiem for a Nun*. Certainly among the major accomplishments of this great novelist has been the sense that his total work presents of movement in time, of the pattern of events. Not only can one with relative ease arrange the novels in the Yoknapatawpha County group in a historical sequence; that sequence is one which encourages the reader to see, defined with vigor and clarity, the existence of a pattern, the presence of some meaning. If indeed, as Steven Marcus has suggested, a great writer acts as the imagination of the actual society in which he lives by formulating an imagined sense of itself for his fellow citizens,[13] if as Mark Schorer suggested of Sinclair Lewis, the writer gives us "a vigorous, perhaps a unique thrust into the imagination of ourselves,"[14] then William Faulkner of Mississippi, great-grandson of Colonel William C. Falkner of Mississippi and *The White Rose of Memphis,* in embodying in his vast chronicle his fellow southerners' sense of themselves, found that sense so intimately bound up with the past of his region that, if his testimony is trustworthy, the southerner of Faulkner's generation could not truly imagine himself independent of his history.

Let us look briefly at some of Faulkner's efforts that body forth that sense of the past, remembering that among American novelists Faulkner is one of the most inveterate experimenters in form.

The first of these examinations of the relationship of past and present in Faulkner's work will be *Light in August;* it is strongly reminiscent of Ellen Glasgow's *The Sheltered Life.* (The novels appeared in the same year, 1932, but I am not suggesting any direct influence.) I am referring to that strand of *Light in August* which deals with the Reverend Gail Hightower, the son of a pacifist, an abolitionist, and "a phantom . . . who had been a minister without a church and a soldier without an enemy, and who in defeat had combined the two and become a doctor, a surgeon."[15] His grandfather had been a Confederate soldier, and as a child and a young man, Hightower had been profoundly moved by tales told him by his father and by a Negro woman about his grandfather's death during the Civil War. Hightower becomes in his own mind a kind of ghostly embodiment of that grandfather, reliving in his imagination his grandfather's glorious end when he was killed in a cavalry raid in Jefferson. In actual fact his grandfather was killed in a raid on a hen house and probably by a Confederate soldier's wife, but this fact has been converted into a completely heroic action in Hightower's memory. He goes to a seminary and studies for the ministry, seeking a profession in which he can find asylum from the world. He marries a woman whom he does not love because she can influence the authorities in the church to secure a call for him to Jefferson, where his grandfather had died. There his sermons are half-mad rhapsodies on the last cavalry charge of his grandfather. For him his church, his congregation, and his wife, as well as everything else in the present, are meaningless. He is held in a kind of permanent suspension from the actual world, while reality becomes for him "the wild bugles and the clashing sabres and the dying thunder of hooves."[16] His frustrated wife is driven to promiscuity and suicide, and he is shut out in disgrace from his church, but he lives on in Jefferson, a flaccid, fat, breathing corpse.

In a long introspective passage near the end of the novel, after he has tried to reenter the world of men by assisting Byron Bunch, Lena Grove, and Joe Christmas, "with this last left of honor and pride and life. . . . He hears above his heart the thunder increase, myriad and drumming. Like a long sighing of wind in trees it begins, then they sweep into sight, borne now upon a cloud of phantom dust. They rush past, forwardleaning in the saddles, with brandished arms, beneath whipping ribbons from slanted and eager lances; with tumult and soundless yelling they sweep past like a tide whose crest is jagged with wild heads of horses and the brandished arms of men like the crater of the world in explosion."[17] And Hightower remains what, in a moment of honesty, he has known himself to be, "a charlatan preaching worse than heresy . . . offering instead of the crucified shape of pity and love, a swaggering and unchastened bravo killed with a shotgun in a peaceful henhouse."[18]

In *Light in August* Faulkner, through Gail Hightower, wrote intensely about the destructive effects of a deep absorption with a falsified and sentimentalized past; in *Absalom, Absalom!* he set out to explore the joint questions of what history is and how we can know it and understand it and how the southern consciousness can respond to the terrible facts of the southern past. This task is accomplished in one of the most complex novels ever constructed by an American. It is a story filled with action, event, and character, with a complicated plot, containing events enough for a 1,500–page novel, if it were told in orthodox scenes. But the story comes to us piecemeal and out of chronological sequence, largely through conversations, reconstructions, and dialectical commentary by a few people, almost none of whom are actually aware of the truth of the events which they describe. The story itself is ostensibly the record of Thomas Sutpen, a poor white from Virginia, who is attempting to create in Mississippi his equivalent of a great southern family dynasty.

The forward action in *Absalom, Absalom!* occurs in a dormitory room at Harvard in 1910, when Quentin Compson, of Mississippi, and his roommate Shreve McCannon, of Canada, who knows nothing at all about the South, are attempting through conversation and speculation to reconstruct the history of events that made up the life of Thomas Sutpen. The basis of Quentin's account is his very limited experience, his own speculation, and narratives told him by Miss Rosa Coldfield and by his father, together with reported accounts by his grandfather General Compson. The significant story is the one which occurred in the past, and the forward story in the present is an attempt to understand that story. Faulkner here is employing to some extent the structure of the detective story, a form he himself used from time to time. In the detective story a high premium is placed on the interpretation of the past and on understanding the indications available in the present of what had happened in the past. The forward action of the detective story consists of the activities of the detective and his assistants as they discover clues which point to the true story of the crime that occurred in the past. When at last they are able to reconstruct that story, their task is complete. Hence the detective story is usually epistemological in its concern. *Absalom, Absalom!* is like the detective story in its persistent attempt to understand the past from partially perceived fragments surviving out of it. Its following of the formula of the detective story is sporadic, and its present seekers after an understanding of the past finally behave like neither detectives nor prosecuting attorneys, but like artists or sociologists.

Quentin and Shreve represent two radically different ways of looking at the data of history. Each of them identifies with a different character in the past, and each finds a different answer to the riddle that he is asking about the meaning of these events. Quentin's identification is with Henry Sutpen, Thomas's son, who kills his half-brother Charles Bon, who has a trace of Negro blood, at the gates to Sutpen's Hundred, lest Charles marry Henry's sister. Quentin's identification is intense, very personal, and larger than life. Shreve, uninvolved and unfamiliar with the region, makes a logical construct that centers in a social meaning. Mr. Compson in the novel says: "We have a few old mouth-to-mouth tales; we exhume from old trunks and boxes and drawers letters without salutation or signature, in which men and women who once lived and breathed are now merely initials and nicknames out of some now incomprehensible affection which sound to us like Sanskrit or Chocktaw; we see dimly people, the people in whose living blood and seed we ourselves lay dormant waiting, in this shadowy attenuation of time possessing now heroic proportions, performing their acts of simple passion and simple violence, impervious to time and inexplicable."[19] This describes both the fragmentary nature of the factual data and the intensely personal nature of Quentin's involvement with it, for he is seed of these people's seed, bone of these people's bone. They loom for him as they did for his father as vast phantasmagorical figures who define self and sin and society. The black shadow of slavery and of racial injustice is his, and these people out of his past have for him a deep moral meaning which transcends their social history and gives their story a deep, almost Grecian tragic quality.

Shreve McCannon, ignorant of the South, studying to be a physician, sees in the narrative that Quentin tells about the House of Sutpen not a retelling of a Greek tragedy but a symbol of the South's social history. He approaches it with logic and reason, not with intense personal identification. He carefully pieces together the data in much the same way that a scientific historian would. From time to time in the dialectical commentary of these two upon the narrative, they seem to speak with a single voice, but at those times—and they are numerous—when each speaks in his own person and with his own voice, it is Quentin who is tormented by his past as he examines the inglorious history of Sutpen's ambition, and it is Shreve who constructs out of that ambition a social history of the region. In one sense Shreve's reconstruction of that social history is correct, but it is, as Faulkner remarked in a comment made during his period at the University of Virginia, only one of thirteen ways of looking at a blackbird,[20] and it is not the particular way that gives *Absalom, Absalom!* its power or makes it one of Faulkner's greatest creative imaginations or that is responsible for the elaborately complex and challenging structure he gave the narrative. That power, that success, and that structure come from Faulkner's sense of these beings as more than pieces in a puzzle of social history, as more than data to be categorized and tabulated, for above and behind Faulkner's view is a sense of order and justice, a world of human values against which man may try himself, a justice which strikes a final balance regardless of the immediate outcome. Hence for Faulkner, whether viewed as the social history of the South or as the effort of the historian to reconstruct that history, the events of the past are means toward an end, and they create finally a fable rather than a fact, a fable that remains meaningful in terms of what it says about man rather than in what man says about it.

Shreve, the historian, and Quentin, the involved artist, collaborate to reconstruct a representative history of their region in relation to slavery, the Civil War, and Reconstruction, and each is essential to the other. Quentin must supply the data out of his own experience, and it is upon that data that Shreve's historical construction must rest. Yet Shreve's historical construction teaches Quentin to see and accept the reality of his past. In a sense it forces Quentin's knowledge of his past out of romanticizing, sentimentalizing, and demonizing and makes him recognize the role that Negro slavery has played in the history of his region and the immense guilt which that role assigns to the inhabitants of the region. Seldom have the materials and techniques of fiction been used with greater skill and intensity in an effort to present simultaneously two seemingly opposed views of what history is and how history works. At the end of *Absalom, Absalom!* the examination of the past has forced Quentin Compson to a recognition of himself and to some degree a recognition of his and everyman's complicity in human history. That that complicity will prove to be more than he can endure is a part of another story which Faulkner had already told in *The Sound and the Fury*.

These are casual remarks about works which have been examined repeatedly and in great detail, as most of Faulkner's work has been, and my intention has not been to cast new light upon these works but simply to indicate the extent to which this greatest of twentieth-century southern writers has worked with vigor, courage, and ingenuity to create in the modern novel a complex awareness of the interaction of past and present and to assert that in so doing, he was following a course frequently taken by others in his region.

In Robert Penn Warren's most successful single piece of fiction, *All the King's Men,* the protagonist Jack Burden, when he was a graduate student, had worked with the manuscript papers of Cass Mastern, who had died in the Confederate Army during the Civil War. In the fourth chapter of that book, Warren gives a long account of the facts that Jack Burden uncovered in his research into the strange story of Cass Mastern's life. When he was a graduate student, he had been unable to come to know Cass Mastern as a human being and to understand what his life had meant, so he had abandoned the project. He could read the words, but Warren asked, "how could he be expected to understand them? They could only be words to him, for to him the world then was an accumulation of items, odds and ends of things like the broken and misused and dust-shrouded things gathered in a garret. Or it was a flux of things before his eyes (or behind his eyes) and one thing had nothing to do, in the end, with anything else."[21]

The facts of the Cass Mastern story are known to any reader of the novel. It is the story of a man who hates the institution of slavery within which he lives and finally frees his slaves, who falls in love with another man's wife, then plots a murder, and finally dies in the Civil War, in his death expiating somehow his sin. This particular story out of the past comes to have for Jack Burden, working expediently and cynically in the political machine of Willie Stark, a peculiar meaning, which finally he summarizes after he reviews it in the light of his own experiences. He says,

Cass Mastern lived for a few years and in that time he learned that the world is all of one piece. He learned that the world is like an enormous spider web and if you touch it, however lightly, at any point, the vibration ripples to the remotest perimeter and the drowsy spider feels the tingle and is drowsy no more but springs out to fling the gossamer coils about you who have touched the web and then eject the black, numbing poison under your hide. It does not matter whether or not you meant to brush the web of things. Your happy foot or your wing may have brushed it ever so lightly, but what happens always happens and there is the spider, bearded black and with his great faceted eyes glittering like mirrors in the sun, or like God's eye, and the fangs dripping.[22]

Warren's introduction of this historical retrospect given through the memory of one of the characters in the present is in certain ways like "The Deep Past" section of Ellen Glasgow's *The Sheltered Life* and is typical of the inability of the southern writer to look at events outside the dimension of time. This need is peculiarly present in Robert Penn Warren. Without the Cass Mastern story, there would be no way, short of direct auctorial statement, for him to make clear, as he does, that we live in a world of interrelated responsibilities and that there is a moral order in that world which cannot finally be set aside. Time and guilt and expiation, complicity and responsibility are all so intimately tied together in Warren's view of things that there is no way to separate them. The result of the total action is that the protagonist at the end of the story, which on the surface is an account of politics in Louisiana in 1939, recognizes that he and Anne cannot live apart from all the anguish and confusion of history. He says, "I tried to tell her how if you could not accept the past and its burden there was no future, for without one there cannot be the other, and how if you could accept the past you might hope for the future, for only out of the past can you make the future." Both he and Anne then "shall go out of the house and go into the convulsion of the world, out of history into history and the awful responsibility of Time."[23]

Warren, in his next book *World Enough and Time* (1950), attempts a structural and stylistic tour de force that continues something of the same fundamental structural pattern that had existed between Jack Burden and the Cass Mastern story and between poet and balladeer in Warren's early poem *The Ballad of Billie Potts*. In both cases a commenting and mediating voice located in the present deals with an event located in the past and, in a pattern somewhat reminiscent of *Absalom, Absalom!*, attempts to commune with the past and discover not only its facts but its meaning. In *World Enough and Time* Warren is dealing with the celebrated Beauchamp-Sharp murder case, which had proved a fruitful subject for Edgar Allan Poe, Charles Fenno Hoffman, William Gilmore Simms, and several other American writers. In this case, however, he maintains an auctorial stance in 1950 and discusses the problems of constructing the past out of the existing documents surviving from it, sharing from time to time with the reader the problems which as author he confronts. The result is an elaborate and intricate interweaving of two time levels and a concern with the problem of knowing the past and translating its facts into a coherent narrative and finally with the issue of what that past means when its facts are translated.

Warren follows his sources with a reasonable closeness except for changing a few names but seldom changing them enough to keep us, if we are familiar with the Beauchamp-Sharp case, from recognizing who the characters are. For example, Jeroboam Beauchamp becomes Jeremiah Beaumont, but the pattern of his life, his marriage to Rachel Jordan, his participation in the political struggle between adherents of the New Court and the Old Court in Kentucky, his avenging the early sexual betrayal of his wife by his close friend Fort, and his subsequent trial for Fort's murder are all fairly faithful to the recorded historical events. The real Jeroboam Beauchamp was hanged, whereas Jeremiah Beaumont is rescued in a series of elaborate maneuverings, primarily because Warren's narrative demands that he come to a recognition of the fact that he shares complicity and guilt and the meaning of time with all men.

In *World Enough and Time* Warren is attempting to write a novel of ideas, and the central concerns are with the relationship of man to time, to guilt, and to complicity. In order to discuss these ideas as ideas, he has selected a peculiar narrative stance which many of his readers feel is a challenging and exciting effort but which finally fails of complete success. The novel speaks to us as a consciously made work of art, and our awareness of the hand of the maker at numerous points throughout it is a weakness in the book, a weakness which Warren was perhaps attempting to acknowledge and to persuade us to set aside in giving it the subtitle "A Romantic Novel," for such a designation warns us that the traditional standards of verisimilitude and immediate acceptance of the authenticity of statement have surrendered to other purposes.

Yet his concern with documents and data, so like that of *Absalom, Absalom!*, is interesting. As the book opens he says, "I can show you what is left. After the pride, passion, agony, and bemused aspiration, what is left is in our hands. Here are the scraps of newspaper, more than a century old, splotched and yellowed and huddled together in a library, like November leaves abandoned by the wind, damp and leached out, back of the stables or in a fenced corner of a vacant lot. Here are the diaries, the documents, and the letters, yellowed too, bound in neat bundles with tape so stiffened and tied that it parts almost unresisting at your touch. Here are the records of what happened in that courtroom, all the words taken down. Here is the manuscript he himself wrote, day after day, as he waited in his cell, telling his story."[24] So this book is thoroughly in keeping with one of the major efforts of contemporary southern novelists to inquire into the matter of how we can get back with any accuracy into the past and what it means when we arrive.

This kind of inquiry Warren continues in *Brother to Dragons*, in which the poet, called RPW, carries on a discourse with Thomas Jefferson—that is, with the ghost of Thomas Jefferson in the present (1953)—about an event which occurred during Jefferson's lifetime and which Warren imagines Jefferson's seeing as forcing him to recognize the darkness and the evil inherent in human history. In this work, the dialogue is between two people not themselves a part of the action in any significant way; one is involved intimately in the action through family and other relationships, and the other is an outside, skeptical, and inquiring voice—that of the poet. The two try to piece together what an event lost in the mist of time means about the universal condition of man. The ghosts of the participants in that event—the brutal butchering of a slave by Jefferson's nephew in Kentucky—join the dialogue, recount events, and themselves try to understand it and find its meaning. The reconciliation, which Jefferson finds difficult, between the "glory" represented by the Declaration of Independence and the evil inherent in the nature of man, is finally expressed by the ghost of his sister, who has discovered it in suffering and in love:

> For whatever hope we have is not by repudiation,
> And whatever health we have is not by denial,
> But in confronting the terror of our condition.[25]

Once more the problem of human guilt shared by all men, the loss of innocence, which is inevitable in the passage of time, the concern with time and its flow as the crucial events in human history, and the complicity of all men which must be recognized along with their inevitable interrelatedness are underscored, as they are in most of Warren's works. In this long poem, which deals with the past with great accuracy, he found his most successful strategy for stating the enduring human lessons to be found in the past.

In 1955 Warren published *Band of Angels,* a story which explores the nature of human freedom through an account of Amantha Starr, the illegitimate daughter of a slaveowner by one of his slaves, who was raised as his daughter, only upon his death to be discovered to be an unmanumitted slave and sold. The book's action occurs along the Mississippi and in New Orleans just before and during the Civil War. It has unmistakable debts for some of its themes, characters, and actions to Harriet Beecher Stowe's *Uncle Tom's Cabin* and to John W. De Forest's *Miss Ravenel's Conversion from Secession to Loyalty.* Its plot is complex and highly melodramatic; its action moves very rapidly; and its general shape is that of a melodramatic historical novel almost of the sort we would have expected to find at the turn of the century, during the heyday of the historical romance. However, this melodrama, which stretches its credibility beyond the breaking point from time to time, is a consciously calculated device to make a fable whose parts explore issues of individual identity, of guilt, of freedom, and of the relationship of the individual to an exterior and controlling world. And Amantha Starr broods upon her position in her society and in the world with a kind of puzzling and questioning self-knowledge and self-scrutiny that is far more intense than one would normally expect to find in the sort of historical romance the book, at least on the surface, appears to be.

Walter Sullivan, in an examination of the novel that is essentially hostile, considers it a failure, because, he asserts, Warren has embraced an existential point of view in presenting his character, and that existential point of view is false to the thought processes that Amantha Starr would have had at the time of the action of the story.[26] I share Sullivan's belief that *Band of Angels* fails as a novel, but I believe that its failure comes not from "the existential peril," which I do not feel that Warren actually shares, but from the fact that he has subordinated the story and the characters to a plot structure which manipulates the action and the reactions of characters in order to make statements about the nature of freedom—essentially the statement that freedom simply does not exist in this world and that freedom ultimately consists of, at best, our choice of the person or the thing to which we yield it.

From *All the King's Men* through this sequence of books—*World Enough and Time, Brother to Dragons,* and *Band of Angels*—Warren had been attempting to explore basically the same issues about man, history, and time and to assert essentially the same position, that of the interlocking complicity and responsibility of all individuals and the inescapable guilt we all share. But after *All the King's Men,* in which he had a narrator given to extensive speculation and commentary upon the meaning of events, one who for all his brashness ultimately does manage to state the positions that Warren wants us to take, he has used a variety of strategies in order to force the actions and events of his story to assume for the reader the pattern of interpretation which he intended. In *World Enough and Time,* he serves himself as author to comment on the action and to be assured that we understand it as he meant; here, too, he attempts to engage the reader with him in the process of reconstruction and interpretation. In *Brother to Dragons* he serves as commentator along with the ghost of characters related to the action of the story, so that a dialectical series of statements about meaning and theme can accompany the action; indeed, that dialogue proves to be the frame within which the action of the story takes place. And in *Band of Angels,* despite the presence of a first-person narrator who can ask such up-to-date questions as, "Who am I?" and *"If I could only be free,* I used to think, free from the lonely nothingness of being only yourself when the world flees away, and free from the closing walls that would crush you to nothingness,"[27] the essential statement does not reside in these interior and anguished meditations of the protagonist but in the pattern of events, melodramatic and overdrawn, which make up the action of the story. Warren has attempted four different ways of modifying the novel in order to discuss the past and its relevance to the present and to see to it that a predominant idea is not lost upon his readers. Only one of them is a complete success, but the experimental efforts are interesting and instructive, not only for what they tell us about the novel of ideas, but particularly for what they demonstrate about Warren's pervasive concerns with history.

We shall not explore the problems of time and history and their role in Warren's work beyond this point, with one exception, although he has continued to be concerned with these matters. In the late 1950s and early 1960s, however, his concern also turned to sociological statements and essays about history such as *Segregation: The Inner Conflict of the South* (1956), *The Legacy of the Civil War: Meditations on the Centennial* (1961), and *Who Speaks for the Negro?* (1965). That these concerns with history and the past did not end with these nonfiction books is demonstrated by the reemergence of one of his favorite themes in his historical novel of the Civil War *Wilderness* (1961). By the time Warren came to write this book he was far enough from the early southern Agrarian roots which had motivated such works as his biography of John Brown and his early poetry and fiction that now his protagonist is an immigrant Jewish boy who has come to America to fight for freedom as a tribute to the liberal heritage of his dead father. This boy, Adam Rosensweig, has a club foot, a rather obvious symbol of his imperfection and of the inheritance of guilt and ineptness. He wishes to join the Union Army but is unable to do so because of his deformity and becomes a sutler serving the Union Army. In the progress of this work he kills a man, meets a girl, loses everything he has, including both his companions—a Negro who is a deserter from the Northern army and a vicious North Carolinian who has fled because he had defended a Negro slave against an unjust charge. The boy finally comes to know his own identity, to recognize that all of us are inextricably in history, that history is another name for the common human condition, that to escape history means simply to withdraw from your role in the human race, that even from those who have done terrible wrongs, "History needed forgiveness."[28] Early in the story an elderly and wise uncle, who has made a great success in America but whose son has died in the Union Army, tells Adam, "If you have stopped worshipping God all you can fall back on is History. I suppose I worship History, since a man has to worship something. I suppose I am not wise enough not to let worshipping History make me ironical." This uncle also tells Adam, "You know, there's always a reason. That's what History is—the reason for things. That's why it can take the place of God. God being the reason for things, too. . . . It's just that God is tired of taking the blame. He's going to let History take the blame for a while." And he defines history as "the agony people have to go through so that things will turn out as they would have turned out anyway." And in a figure as old for Warren as Cass Mastern's narrative, Adam "felt a thousand filmy strands being cast over him, binding him, netting him down."[29] *Wilderness* is a minor work, though it avoids many of the excesses that Warren's fiction in recent years has suffered from; yet even in this minor work, Warren is trying to define the Civil War as a meaningful conflict for freedom, and his concern with the nature of history is still pervasive.

I would like to point to only one other southern novel,

this a quite recent and very famous one, *The Confessions of Nat Turner* by William Styron. In this novel Styron, certainly one of the most impressive talents currently working in the novel in America, turns to race, the major concern of the southern novelist in our time, and reconstructs the series of events which occurred during the uprising in Southampton County, Virginia, in August of 1831, when a group of slaves led by Nat Turner began a revolt which ultimately ended in their defeat, capture, and execution. While he was in jail, Turner dictated to his court-appointed lawyer an account of the insurrection. This confession was widely published at the time of his trial and after. Using it as a basis Styron has elaborated into a book of 429 pages the confessions of Nat Turner as a kind of formal meditation. In his note at the beginning of the book Styron says, "The relativity of time allows us elastic definitions: the year 1831 was, simultaneously, a long time ago and only yesterday. Perhaps the reader will wish to draw a moral from this narrative but it has been my own intention to try to re-create a man and his era, and to produce a work that is less an 'historical novel' in conventional terms than a meditation on history."[30]

Certainly here the attempt to recreate the past in terms of a meaning reaches about as definite a goal as it is likely to accomplish in our time. For both William Styron and the reader stand in the present being invited to look at the inner feelings of a slave insurrectionist in 1831, to understand his motives, to sympathize with his agonies and his passions, and finally to accept the guilt which we as the inheritors of a society bear for the injustices which it heaped upon the slaves who constituted the bedrock upon which it rested. The book has been attacked by a group of black writers who feel that it falsifies their position, demeans the slave, and represents a series of issues that are essentially racist.[31] However, the author has not violated known facts about the actual insurrection—although this statement certainly has been challenged by some of his black critics—but he did allow his imagination substantial freedom within the boundaries of the sparse facts that are known.

The most remarkable aspect of the book is that Styron has found a voice of his own within which to record what must only be the inner feelings rather than the external expressions of Nat Turner, a fact that becomes obvious when the actual dialogue in the book where Turner and his fellow slaves speak a language appropriate to their station and education is examined. Turner, of course, was at least minimally educated; he was a minister and a very devout man, and he knew the Bible well enough for the rhythms and the echoes of the King James version to shape the style in which his confessions are phrased. But there can be no question that Nat Turner as here presented is William Styron's attempt to comprehend the feelings and the passions of a man rather than an attempt to recreate an era resting upon very much historical evidence.

The enormous force which the book brings to bear upon its reader today results from the extent to which it lays upon the shoulders of that reader the heavy burden of his own past. The book is flawed in a number of different ways, to me most notably in Styron's selection of this single point of view and its highly interior consciousness, which is laid before us in a language appropriate to its characters in its rhythm, but not in its complexity and figures. This single point of view creates about all events such an intensity and remoteness that, except on occasion, the social reality within which the Southampton insurrection occurred is at best hazily sketched. I think that it would have been to Styron's advantage to have found somehow a means of giving us a social context against which to view these things. For the pendulum in *The Confessions of Nat Turner*, brilliant achievement though the book is, has swung almost all the way from a view of society to a view of the self in violent opposition to that society.

In one sense *The Confessions of Nat Turner* stands at an extreme from the kind of historical novel that was written by William Gilmore Simms or Mary Johnston, in which the society that individuals create has so dominant a role that the individuals seem to exist as faceless and weak in feeling. In William Styron's novel our contemporary tendencies toward introspection and the private self are so strong that the society, whether of the oppressing white man's world or of the interior and smaller slave hegemony, fades almost into nothingness. Styron's *Confession*, for all its traditional technique, is a thoroughly modern novel, and yet even here the southerner's bondage to the past cannot be escaped.

The temptation has been strong to add to the authors I have considered several others who have written of the past in fresh and challenging ways, and I have been able to resist that temptation only because the space available is very limited and because I think the examples I have chosen demonstrate the point I am trying to make. Among those whose insistent clamor I have had to resist are: T. S. Stribling, particularly *The Forge* (1931), *The Store* (1932), and *Unfinished Cathedral* (1934); Evelyn Scott's *The Wave* (1931); Elizabeth Madox Roberts, particularly *The Time of Man* (1926) and *The Great Meadow* (1930); Caroline Gordon's *None Shall Look Back* (1937) and *Green Centuries* (1941); and very particularly Andrew Lytle's distinguished and challenging work, *The Long Night* (1936), *At the Moon's Inn* (1941), and *The Velvet Horn* (1957).

What this group of novels shows us, I believe, is that the extent to which the past has been obsessively present to the southern writer has not really changed significantly with changing literary fashions but rather has been intensified. Allen Tate, in 1935, said, in a statement that has often been approvingly quoted by most students of southern literature, "From the peculiarly historical consciousness of the Southern writer has come good work of a special order; but the focus of this consciousness is quite temporary. It has made possible a curious burst of intelligence that we get at a crossing of the ways, not unlike, on an infinitesimal scale, the outburst of poetic genius at the end of the sixteenth century when commercial England had already begun to crush feudal England. The Histories and Tragedies of Shakespeare record the death of the old régime and Doctor Faustus gives up feudal order for world power."[32] In 1959 Tate agreed that he had underestimated the energy of this movement,[33] but in actual fact he had not merely underestimated it, for he was quite wrong: the concern of the southerner with history has always been a persistent aspect of southern writing. The backward glance that the South cast toward an old order as it moved into the twentieth century—Tate's particular definition of the moment in history of which he writes—was but an incident in a long chronicle of the southern writers' involvement with their past.

In our time that involvement continues as a distinctive mark of southern fiction. The southern writer of the last fifty years has sought new means of considering man in time and has found him overburdened by the presence in his region of the black man and by the courses of action which that region has taken toward the black man from 1620 to the present. Out of this consideration has emerged a sense of deep guilt and an awareness of the persistence of evil in the world, a sense of our inevitable culpability in the affairs of man, a knowledge that whatever we inherit, like the inheritance of Ike McCaslan in Faulkner's "The Bear," is tainted by the means by which it was originally earned. These awarenesses have made the southern writer seek upon the altar of art a means of expiating the guilt of his society. And since to a greater extent than writers from any other part of the nation he has special love for and understanding of the importance of society as society and a keen awareness of the interaction of the individual with society, the southern writer has attempted in many and various ways to fashion out of his acknowledgment of guilt and his pervasive sense of evil, through the darkness, terror, and despair of much twentieth-century writing, some catharsis for his fear and pity and some sense of man's responsibility to others.

The religions of the world have often employed the scapegoat to bring peace to the soul and to awaken the spirit to right impulses and noble actions; the sins of the group are loaded symbolically upon the scapegoat who, through his sacrifice, expiates them. In a sense the southern writer has served as such a scapegoat for his fellow Americans, for in his explorations of the meaning and nature of the past, he has taken their guilt upon himself and has dramatized it. Thus he has borne in some imaginative sense the sins of us all. In a nation which has made a fetish out of existence in the here and now, which sees the past as something dead and the future as something to be created fresh and totally new, the southern writer, overwhelmed with his sense of guilt, oppressed with his sense of irony, and in every sense aware of the common complicity of man, has said to the world at large, as Hegel had said in the nineteenth century, "History has shape, history has meaning, and, though at different times we may embody it in our works of art in different forms and by different methods, we cannot and indeed must not ignore it. For we ignore it only at our own peril and the peril of the society of which we are a part." And so the southern writer says to all of us, in the words of Jack Burden from Warren's *All the King's Men*, "Let us go into the convulsion of the world, out of history into history and the awful responsibility of Time."[34]

5
"The Cosmic Clock of History"

> ... we seek to determine the position of our present within ... a temporal framework, to tell by the cosmic clock of history what the time is. —Karl Mannheim, *Essays on the Sociology of Knowledge*
>
> In the one ... Space is more or less given, and the action is built up in time; in the other, Time is assumed, and the action is a static pattern, continuously redistributed and reshuffled, in Space. —Edwin Muir, *The Structure of the Novel*
>
> In America ... man did not feel a disorientation in his sense of time, but a liberation from time. Even if Jefferson had declared that the study of history should be basic for the education of the free citizen, space replaced time as the prime category for that citizen; and man, moving ever westward, was redeemed from the past. ...
> —Robert Penn Warren, *Democracy and Poetry*[1]

I HAVE attempted, by examining a very selected—but I believe representative—body of southern fiction, to show a consistency in their concern with the historical past on the part of novelists in the southeastern United States through most of the literary history of the region. The past, I have argued, is inescapable to the southerner, and he sees that past, not in Nietzschean terms of endless replication through each individual of the universal racial experience, but in Hegelian terms of pattern, of change, in which ultimate meanings are functions of the process and not of the individual events. Hence, of the coordinates of time and space within which events occur, time assumes for the southern novelist the major role, despite the fact that both coordinates are, of necessity, present in any verbal representation of human action.

May I digress for a moment to illustrate my point with two nonsouthern novels well known to us all? Herman Melville's *Moby-Dick* is a spatial representation of certain cosmic questions. "I take SPACE to be the central fact to man born in America," declared Charles Olson, in his brilliant study of *Moby-Dick, Call Me Ishmael,* and he added "I spell it large because it comes large here. Large, and without mercy."[2] Moby Dick is, the sailors declare, "ubiquitous and immortal," and the ocean on which the *Pequod* sails is not in time but is eternity. Melville works hard to give his readers a sense that the true action of the novel belongs to primeval prehistory, frequently using the present tense, giving his characters symbolic single names—Ahab, Ishmael, Queequeg, Starbuck—and letting the major characters speak an Elizabethan rhetoric. The voyage is a quest, eternal and endlessly repeated, for answers to cosmic riddles, and in that quest Ahab discards the accumulated knowledge gained in history—the pipe, the razors, the quadrant—and confronts the universe in the most primitive possible form, shouting his defiance in ritual terms—"*Ego non baptizo te in nomine patris, sed in nomine diaboli.*" Joseph Frank has declared one of the characteristics of modern writing to be the effort to create through form "a timeless unity" in which "historical time does not exist [and] the imagination . . . sees the actions and events of a particular time merely as the bodying forth of eternal prototypes."[3] By such a standard *Moby-Dick* is thoroughly modern.

In contrast Nathaniel Hawthorne's *The Scarlet Letter* is a work that powerfully emphasizes time rather than space. It is not merely that Boston in the 1640s was a constricted and isolated place surrounded by wilderness and danger; the action moves forward in time with all the inevitable urgency with which Hester Prynne's pregnancy had advanced to create the initial situation. Hawthorne is keenly aware of the social and religious nature of the age he describes, and he utilizes the characteristics of the

1640s with precision in advancing the movement of his plot. In one clear sense he has written an historical novel, and although he is certainly interested in some eternal laws of human character and morality, he examines them by showing their application in a definite time and a fixed space, and in his concluding chapter he speculates on what Hester would have done and how she would have developed in other times. It is not surprising that Hawthorne is often regarded as the New England writer who is most nearly southern in his attitudes and is most like Faulkner.[4]

The essential differences between these symbolic novelists, Melville and Hawthorne, have been frequently explored,[5] but in their views of history and in their differing uses of time and space, perhaps the real key is to be found. Melville explores meanings out of time, out of history, and his vast Pacific is in an eternally unchanging time. Thus his work takes on mythic or archetypal dimensions. Hawthorne knows and respects New England history, and he finds his meanings in events in time. Despite his impatience with the lack of moral depth in Scott's themes, Hawthorne saw man in history as Scott had, and he often wrote historical fiction.

"The historical novel is, so to speak, the 'natural,' as it is the largely unexamined, form for the English and European novel in the nineteenth century," Steven Marcus has said.[6] On the contrary, in America it was only in the South that such a statement could be considered true,[7] and it has been the absence in the mainstream of the American novel of a consistent and necessitating concern with history and time, with society and political issues that has in part resulted in a special quality in the American novel which Richard Chase identified with romance in his perceptive but very incomplete study *The American Novel and Its Tradition*.[8] And the situation has not changed significantly in the twentieth century. As Philip Rahv has wisely observed, "To some people it appears as though the past, all of it together with its gods and sacred books, were being ground to pieces in the powerhouse of change. . . . One way certain intellectuals have found of coping with their fear is to deny historical time and induce in themselves through aesthetic and ideological means a sensation of mythic time—the eternal past of ritual."[9] The modern American novel tends to deal with this "eternal"—in that it is timeless—past of mythic time or, as most often happens, it seeks in the solipsistic depths of the private self the only meaning that the novelist values.

But the word *myth* is a dangerous one to introduce into a discussion of southern writing. The historians have written of the myths—they usually see several—of southern history, meaning the views southerners have taken of themselves, the past, and their problems.[10] In this sense, a myth is an erroneous belief to be corrected. In another and rather loose sense, *myth* is used as roughly synonymous with *archetype,* and to the degree that any piece of writing repeats actions common to recurrent human experience, it tends to be "mythic." *Myth* is fairly widely used in the sense made popular by critics who admire Mircea Eliade, whose theories may be crudely summarized as seeing man constructing myths that redeem time and the human condition.[11] Lewis P. Simpson, in *The Dispossessed Garden,* and Walter Sullivan, in *A Requiem for the Renascence,* have argued for a view of the southern experience and southern literature as sacramental acts, shoring up Truth against the gnosticism of the present age.[12] By such an interpretation literature ultimately becomes a religious act, and the distinctiveness of southern writing rests not on its view of social structures or the facts of history but upon the religious orientation of the region. The history considered by such writers tends to be like that of Nietzsche's replication or of Carl Jung's archetypes. Without wishing to question the idea that the religious nature of southern life is an important element in the power of southern literary expression, I would question the centrality of the sacramental to the accomplishments of our best writers. For, it seems to me, equally important has been the southerner's concern with national and regional history and with historical time.

The southerner has been noted for the particularity and the concreteness of his imagination. Robert Penn Warren, for example, has remarked on the southerner's "instinctive fear . . . that the massiveness of experience, the concreteness of life, will be violated . . . the fear of abstraction."[13] Southern literary critics have tended to value the particular, to be superb practical critics and poor or casual theoreticians. The emphasis of the New Critics was on "the poem *per se*," the autonomous, unique work of art. A novelist like Andrew Lytle, who became enamored of myth while he was writing *The Velvet Horn*, still shows in his criticism, collected in *The Hero with the Private Parts* and dealing predominantly with historical fiction, this same typical southern particularity. "In fiction," he says, "the action must be put in a recognizable place and society."[14] The result of this sense of the sanctity of the concrete is that the southerner is not really interested in an abstract past; he is interested in *his* past, and he can usually pinpoint time, place, and familial relationship to the level of the third cousin. The essentially Calvinistic Protestantism of the South certainly has an important role to play in the southern writer's sense of guilt, but the guilt he feels and expresses is seldom universalized and almost never abstract; it is immediate, historical, concrete, and it deals with men and actions.

I believe one of the distinctive aspects of the southern mind is its comparative freedom from a belief in geographical solutions to pressing problems. One of the tendencies of mobile, modern America is restless movement. If things don't work out, move on, or move elsewhere. The frontier, physically speaking, is an arena for new actions by nameless actors who come out of nowhere, abide awhile, and then move on. The southerner, on the other hand, confronted by a pressing problem inquires how it came to be and what has been tried for its solution, and then he recalls what Uncle Silas did in a similar situation, and—it must be admitted—all too often works out a way of living with the problem still unsolved.

In this respect Thomas Wolfe is an interesting illustration of both North and South. Linked within him were two opposing strains, his father's Pennsylvania blood and his mother's Carolina mountain-man strain. He was very much like his protagonist Eugene Gant, in *Look Homeward, Angel,* who was, he said: "The fusion of the two strong egotisms, Eliza's inbrooding and Gant's expanding outward." Eliza, his mother, was one of the "time-devouring Pentlands," a mountain family, tied to place, to clan, to history. His father "had the passion of the true wanderer," who near the end of his life made a 9,000–mile trip to California, and looked on his return as being "to the bleak bare prison of the hills," after "the final flare of the old hunger that had once darkened in the small grey eyes, leading a boy into new lands...."[15] And Wolfe himself was sufficiently his father's son to be through most of his short life a far-wanderer, eternally restless, eternally lonely, trying to define the vast geography of his land, the lonely sweep of continent, the rush of rivers, and the towering peaks of mountains. And yet the South burned in his blood and flooded his memory, and from his mother came the legends of family and the past which were to be woven richly into the fabric of his work. Each of his novels he began with a long historical introduction, usually beginning at the Civil War. Editors, wisely or not, deleted these historical prologues, but the ten chapters of the incomplete *The Hills Beyond,* posthumously published, shows one of the directions in which Wolfe's imagination moved. Two of his best shorter works are "Chickamauga," a short story about the Civil War, and "The Web of Earth," a novella based on his mother's family reminiscences.

The conflict of time and space was more evenly balanced in Wolfe than it was in most southern writers, yet time was the single most nearly philosophical concept in his work. In *The Story of a Novel,* Wolfe's single attempt at an essay in criticism, he carefully describes what he is attempting to do with time:

> There are three time elements inherent in the material. The first . . . was an element of actual present time, an element which carried the narrative forward, which represented characters and events as living in the present and moving forward into an immediate future. The second time element was of past time, one which represented these same characters as acting and being acted upon by all the accumulated impact of man's experience so that each moment of their lives was conditioned not only by what they experienced in that moment, but by all that they had experienced up to that moment . . . . there was a third [time element] which I conceived as being time immutable, the time of rivers, mountains, oceans, and the earth; a kind of eternal and unchanging universe of time against which would be projected the transience of man's life, the bitter briefness of his day.[16]

It should be noted that these concepts of time are essentially linear—or at least the first two are—that they are in ceaseless motion, and that they are not cyclical. Repeatedly in Wolfe's work sensory stimuli call up memories of the past with great precision, but they remain memories; the past is, for him, always "far and lost." This view of time is different from Proust's, in which he gives us a sense of time by rising above it and showing us "snapshots of the characters 'motionless in a moment of vision' at different stages in their lives." Proust does this by rising out of the present into what he calls "pure time."[17] Faulkner, for whom also time is usually linear, except in mythic experiments like *A Fable,*[18] creates, like

Proust, characters "motionless in a moment of vision" in his frequent scenes of frozen action.[19] Ellen Glasgow, too, was fascinated with time, as my earlier discussion of *The Sheltered Life* shows. When Margaret Church wrote *Time and Reality*, in which she studied time in contemporary fiction, she examined Bergson, Proust, Joyce, Woolf, Aldous Huxley, Mann, Kafka, and Sartre; but only Wolfe and Faulkner, of American novelists, seemed sufficiently concerned with time to warrant her attention.[20] Hans Meyerhoff, in *Time in Literature,* gives Wolfe serious attention and less than one page to the only other American he examines, F. Scott Fitzgerald.[21] Clearly the southerners' concern with history and the past involves them with theories of time, but not the cyclical or repetitious theories generally associated with myth or with Nietzschean distrust of history.

In his concern with linear time and with the past in terms of sequence of event, the southern novelist remains essentially in the tradition of Hegelian process, as Scott and his successors developed it, and not with the contemporary mythic writers. As Philip Rahv says, "The one essential function of myth . . . is that in merging past and present it releases us from the flux of temporality, arresting change in the timeless, the permanent, the ever-recurrent conceived as 'sacred repetition.' Hence the mythic is the polar opposite of what we mean by the historical, which stands for process, inexorable change . . . ."[22] For better or for worse, the southern novelist has remained wedded to the historical, to process, to inevitable change. However glorified and idealized his view of the past has been from time to time, it has been a view of a specific past, firmly fixed in time, not oblivious of eternity but also not finding its home there. Forced to choose, he will usually elect historicism over myth.

Thus, if my argument is correct, we come full circle. In the dichotomy of historical theory into broadly Hegelian and Nietzschean, we found the dominant American mode Nietzschean, concerned with individual experience and distrustful of the lessons of the past, and the South, in contrast, Hegelian, interested in process, in time, in what the past meant and means. We have seen representative southern writers in every period utilizing the various novelistic modes to say what they have to say, but being consistently concerned with history as event and process and distrustful of the individual outside the context of time and society. Such findings should not really be surprising, for they are in harmony with other qualities of southern writing, with its concreteness, its specificity, its Aristotelian rather than Platonic quality, its urgent sense of time, and its deep respect for tradition. The past has been and still is an inescapable element of the southern mind, not as a myth, not as a retreat, not as a mask, but as a mystery to be understood, as a burden to be borne, as a guilt to be expiated, and as a pattern which can—if anything can—point us to the future.

For the southern writer seems almost instinctively to have always known what Robert Penn Warren magnificently expressed in 1974 in his Jefferson Lecture in the Humanities: "... a society with no sense of the past, with no sense of the human role as significant not merely in experiencing history but in creating it can have no sense of destiny. And what kind of society is it that has no sense of destiny and no sense of self? That has no need or will to measure itself by the record of human achievement and the range of the human endowment?"[23] The southern novelist, I believe to his eternal glory, has worked to keep such a sense of destiny before his region and his nation.

Notes

Chapter 1

The Southern Writer and the Rorschach Test of History

1. Robert Penn Warren, *All The King's Men* (New York, 1946), p. 407.
2. Saul Bellow, *Humboldt's Gift* (New York, 1975), p. 300.
3. F. Scott Fitzgerald, *The Great Gatsby*, in *Three Novels of F. Scott Fitzgerald* (New York, 1953), p. 137.
4. Louis B. Wright, "William Byrd as a Man of Letters," in *The Prose Works of William Byrd of Westover: Narratives of a Colonial Virginian*, ed. Louis B. Wright (Cambridge, Mass., 1966), p. 1. See also Wright's *The First Gentleman of Virginia* (San Marino, Calif., 1940).
5. *Prose Works of Byrd*, pp. 5-6.
6. Reinhold Niebuhr, *The Irony of American History* (New York, 1952), p. 151.
7. G.W.F. Hegel, *The Philosophy of History*, trans. J. Silbee (New York, 1956), pp. 9, 17-18, 25, 29, 56, 79, 457. These are lectures delivered by Hegel in 1830-1831; the translation was first published in 1899.
8. R. G. Collingwood, *The Idea of History* (New York, 1956), pp. 122-26.
9. Hegel, p. 37. He also says, "The State is the Idea of Spirit in the external manifestation of human Will and its Freedom," p. 47.
10. Ralph Waldo Emerson, "The American Scholar," *Emerson: Representative Selections*, ed. Frederic I. Carpenter (New York, 1934), p. 56.
11. Henry D. Thoreau, *Walden*, ed. J. Lyndon Shanley (Princeton, N.J., 1971), p. 333.
12. James Russell Lowell, "The Present Crisis," *Lowell: Representative Selections*, ed. Harry H. Clark and Norman Foerster (New York, 1947), p. 29.
13. Friedrich Nietzsche, *The Use and Abuse of History*, trans. Adrian Collins, The Library of Liberal Arts (Indianapolis, 1957), pp. 5, 11, 36, 51, 57. This essay was originally published in *Unzeitgemässe Betrachtungen (Thoughts Out of Season)*, 1874.
14. Georg Lukács, *The Historical Novel*, trans. Hannah and Stanley Mitchell (Boston, 1963), p. 34.
15. *Coleridge's Miscellaneous Criticism*, ed. T. M. Raysor (London, 1936), pp. 341-42.
16. "The Uses of History in Fiction," a panel discussion by Ralph Ellison, William Styron, Robert Penn Warren, C. Vann Woodward, *Southern Literary Journal* 1 (Spring 1969) : 57-90.
17. Frank Luther Mott, *Golden Multitudes: A History of Best-Selling Books in the United States* (New York, 1947), pp. 64-78; James D. Hart, *The Popular Book in America* (Berkeley, Calif., 1950), pp. 73-80; James T. Hillhouse, *The Waverley Novels and Their Critics* (Minneapolis, Minn., 1936), pp. 10-11.

18. Hegel, too, asserted that "there is no past, no future, but an essential *now*" (p. 79), but he was speaking of an enduring process: "The present form of Spirit comprehends within it all earlier steps. These have indeed unfolded themselves in success independently" (p. 79). There seems no reason to think Cooper had such a concept.

19. See Hawthorne's review of William Gilmore Simms, *Views and Reviews in American Literature, History and Fiction*, in the *Salem Advertiser*, May 2, 1846, reprinted in Randall Stewart, "Hawthorne's Contributions to *The Salem Advertiser*," *American Literature* 5 (January 1934) : 330, where he refers to the Scott-type novel as the "worn out mould . . . which it is time to break up and fling away."

20. A detailed (and perhaps overstated) account of Scott's popularity in the South is in Rollin G. Osterweis, *Romanticism and Nationalism in the Old South* (New Haven, Conn., 1949), pp. 41-53.

21. In Mark Twain, *Life on the Mississippi* (New York, 1923), pp. 332-34, 374-76.

22. William Faulkner, *Go Down Moses* (New York, 1942), pp. 263-81.

23. See William W. Freehling, *Prelude to Civil War: The Nullification Controversy in South Carolina 1816-1836* (New York, 1966), pp. 7-48; Edmund Wilson, *Patriotic Gore: Studies in the Literature of the Civil War* (New York, 1962), pp. 439ff.

24. See J. Carlyle Sitterson, "Edmund Ruffin, Agricultural Reformer and Southern Radical," in his edition of *An Essay on Calcareous Manures* (Cambridge, Mass., 1961), pp. vii-xxxiii.

25. See George C. Rogers, Jr., *Charleston in the Age of the Pinckneys* (Norman, Okla., 1969).

26. Richard Beale Davis, *Intellectual Life in Jefferson's Virginia 1790-1830* (Chapel Hill, N.C., 1964).

Chapter 2

"The Tory Camp Is Now in Sight"

1. The title is from "The Song of Marion's Men" in Simms's *The Partisan;* Stark Young, *So Red the Rose* (New York, 1953), p. 90; Ben Robertson, *Red Hills and Cotton* (New York, 1942), p. 26.

2. "William Gilmore Simms," *De Bow's Review* 29 (1860) : 712.

3. Ibid., p. 708.

4. William R. Taylor, *Cavalier and Yankee: The Old South and American National Character* (New York, 1961), p. 269.

5. Simone Vauthier, "Of Time and the South: The Fiction of William Gilmore Simms," *Southern Literary Journal* 5 (Fall 1972) : 5.

6. Simms, *Views and Reviews of American Literature, History and Fiction*, 1st Ser., ed. C. Hugh Holman (Cambridge, Mass., 1962), pp. 34-35.

7. Ibid., p. 42.

8. See, as illustrative of this view of our history, Charles Olson, *Call Me Ishmael* (New York, 1947); Henry Nash Smith, *Virgin Land: The American West as Symbol and Myth* (Cambridge, Mass., 1950); R.W.B. Lewis, *The American Adam: Innocence, Tragedy and Tradition in the Nineteenth Century* (Chicago, 1955); John G. Cawelti, *Adventure, Mystery, and Romance* (Chicago, 1976), particularly pp. 192-242.

9. Taylor, p. 270.
10. Simms, *The Wigwam and the Cabin*, rev. ed. (New York, 1856), p. 2.
11. [Simms], "Ellet's Women of the Revolution," *Southern Quarterly Review* 17 (1850) : 351-52.
12. Simms, *Mellichampe: A Legend of the Santee*, rev. ed. (New York, 1853), p. 3.
13. Simms, *The Partisan: A Romance of the Revolution*, rev. ed. (New York, 1853), pp. vi-vii.
14. *The Letters of William Gilmore Simms*, ed. Mary C. S. Oliphant, A. T. Odell, T.C.D. Eaves, 5 vols. (Columbia, S.C., 1952-1956), 2 : 315, 319-20, 324-26, 328-29, 336, 338-39, 342-43, 363, 380-81.
15. Vauthier, p. 13.
16. *The Partisan*, p. vii.
17. Donald Davidson, "Introduction," *Letters*, 1: xxxvi-xxxix.
18. See C. Hugh Holman, "Introductions," *Views and Reviews*, pp. xx-xxxvii.
19. *Old Guard Magazine* 5 (January-December 1867) : 1-17, 91-103, 161-76, 241-60, 321-39, 401-21, 481-500, 561-76, 668-81, 731-45, 822-34, 897-935.
20. Simms, *Joscelyn: A Tale of the Revolution* (Columbia, S.C., 1975), p. 305.
21. London, 1830.
22. Simms, "Modern Prose Fiction," *Southern Quarterly Review* 15 (April 1849) : 82. Simms here calls Scott "more perfect, more complete and admirable, than any writer of his age."
23. See Clement Eaton, *Freedom of Thought in the Old South* (Durham, N.C., 1940); David M. Potter, *The Impending Crisis 1848-1861* (New York, 1976), particularly pp. 18-50, 121-44, 448-84.
24. John Greenleaf Whittier, "Massachusetts to Virginia," *John Greenleaf Whittier's Poetry: An Appraisal and Selection*, by Robert Penn Warren (Minneapolis, Minn., 1971), pp. 66-67.
25. Boston, 1847, pp. 32, 34. In a later edition (1864), perhaps partly as a result of Simms's responses, Sabine significantly softened his strictures against South Carolina.
26. *Southern Quarterly Review* 14 (July and October 1848) : 37-77, 261-337.
27. Charleston, S.C., 1853.
28. Review of *Horse-Shoe Robinson* in *Southern Quarterly Review* 22 (July 1852): 203-20.
29. *Letters*, 1 : 319.
30. See C. Hugh Holman, "Introduction," *Views and Reviews*, pp. xxii-xxix.
31. This aspect of Simms's career is dealt with in Taylor, *Cavalier and Yankee*, pp. 271-81, with brilliant perception.
32. John Erskine, *Leading American Novelists* (New York, 1910), p. 177.
33. See John C. Miller, *Triumph of Freedom 1775-1783* (Boston, 1948), 582-95; Willard M. Wallace, *Appeal to Arms: A Military History of the American Revolution* (New York, 1951), 204-45; Paul H. Smith, *Loyalists and Redcoats: A Study in British Revolutionary Policy* (New York, 1972), 79-99, 126-53; John Richard Alden, *The South in the Revolution 1763-1789* (Baton Rouge, La., 1957), pp. 329-89.
34. See Simms, *The Forayers; or, The Raid of the Dog-Days* (New York, 1855), pp. 265-66, for an account of this division.
35. W. A. Schaper, *Sectionalism and Representation in South Carolina* (Washington, D.C., 1901), 1 : 237-463, and Louis B. Wright, *South Carolina: A Bicentennial History* (New York, 1976), which is informed throughout by this sectionalism, but particularly in the Introduction and chapters 5 and 6, pp. 3-15, 82-120.

Notes

36. Miller, pp. 131, 138, 270, 315.
37. Ibid., p. 518.
38. George Bancroft, *History of the United States*, author's last revision (New York, 1897), 5 : 375.
39. Miller, p. 521.
40. Ibid., p. 519.
41. Taylor, p. 262.
42. Georg Lukács, *The Historical Novel*, trans. Hannah and Stanley Mitchell (Boston, 1963), pp. 39-63.
43. Sir Walter Scott, *The Fortunes of Nigel* (Boston, 1923), 1 : vi-vii.
44. See C. Hugh Holman, "William Gilmore Simms's Picture of the Revolution as a Civil War," *Journal of Southern History* 15 (November 1949) : 441-62; reprinted in Holman, *The Roots of Southern Writing* (Athens, Ga., 1972), pp. 35-49.
45. Edward McCrady, *The History of South Carolina in the Revolution 1780-1783* (New York, 1902), p. 734.
46. See, for example, his portrayal of the loyalist Barsfield, modeled on the infamous Col. Thomas Brown, of Augusta, in *Mellichampe*, particularly pp. 2 and 310-14; or old Muggs, in *The Scout; or The Black Riders of the Congaree* (New York, 1854), p. 55.
47. *The History of South Carolina from Its First European Discovery to Its Erection into a Republic* (Charleston, S.C., 1860), p. 179.
48. *The Scout*, pp. 12-13.
49. J. Wesley Thomas, "The German Sources of William Gilmore Simms," in *Anglo-German and American-German Crosscurrents, Volume One*, ed. P. A. Shelley, et al. (Chapel Hill, N.C., 1957), pp. 141-42.
50. See *Letters*, 3 : 224-421, passim, for a record of the writing of *The Forayers* and *Eutaw*.
51. *Letters*, 3 : 421.
52. Simms's notes from this trip are in the Charles Carroll Simms Collection in the South Caroliniana Library at the University of South Carolina. They are transcribed in Appendix A of Miriam J. Shillingsburg's dissertation, "An Edition of William Gilmore Simms's *The Cub of the Panther*" (Univ. of South Carolina, 1969). See also James E. Kibler, Jr., "Simms' Indebtedness to Folk Tradition in 'Sharp Snaffles,'" *Southern Literary Journal* 4 (Spring 1972): 55-86; and "Explanatory Notes," *Voltmeier*, by William Gilmore Simms (Columbia, S.C., 1969), pp. 431-36.
53. Cooke refers to the Civil War as "the late Revolution" in *Surrey of Eagle's-Nest* (New York, 1866), p. 66, and in *The Wearing of the Gray* (New York, 1867), p. 352. He compares Lee with Washington, Mosby with Marion, and Hampton with the rebels against the Crown in the "old Revolution," in *The Wearing of the Gray*, pp. 59, 114, 357. He compares the Federal troops to the Crown bent on subjugating America in *Surrey of Eagle's-Nest*, p. 13, in *Hilt to Hilt* (New York, 1869), p. 150, and in *The Wearing of the Gray*, p. 305.

Chapter 3

"Time . . . The Sheath Enfolding Experience"

1. Robert Penn Warren, *Brother to Dragons: A Tale in Verse and Voices* (New York, 1953), pp. 8-9. The title is from Ellen Glasgow's *The Sheltered Life*.

2. Daniel Aaron, *The Unwritten War: American Writers and the Civil War* (New York, 1973).
3. Ibid., pp. 244-71; Mary Boykin Chesnut, *A Diary from Dixie*, ed. Ben Ames Williams (Boston, 1949). Louis D. Rubin, Jr., in "The Image of an Army," *The Curious Death of the Novel* (Baton Rouge, La., 1967), pp. 183-206, concludes that the Lost Cause has not yet had adequate fictional treatment.
4. An excellent, appreciative discussion of these novels is in Lawrence G. Nelson, "Mary Johnston and the Historic Imagination," in *Southern Writers: Appraisals in Our Time*, ed. R. C. Simonini, Jr. (Charlottesville, Va., 1964), pp. 71-102.
5. Rubin, p. 197.
6. Robert A. Lively, *Fiction Fights the Civil War: An Unpublished Chapter in the Literary History of the American People* (Chapel Hill, N.C., 1957).
7. C. Vann Woodward, *The Burden of Southern History* (Baton Rouge, La., 1960), pp. 170-71.
8. Quoted in ibid., pp. 169-70.
9. Thomas Nelson Page, *The Old Gentleman of the Black Stock* (New York, 1900), pp. vii-viii.
10. See Sheldon Van Auken, "The Southern Historical Novel in the Early Twentieth Century," *Journal of Southern History* 14 (May 1948): 157-91.
11. Thomas Nelson Page, *The Old South: Essays Social and Political* (New York, 1927), p. 5.
12. See F. Garvin Davenport, Jr., *The Myth of Southern History: Historical Consciousness in Twentieth-Century Southern Literature* (Nashville, Tenn., 1970), pp. 23-43.
13. See Lionel Trilling, "Manners, Morals, and the Novel," *The Liberal Imagination* (Garden City, N.Y., 1953), pp. 200-215; Michael Millgate, *American Social Fiction: James to Cozzens* (New York, 1964), pp. 195-212; and particularly James W. Tuttleton, *The Novel of Manners in America* (Chapel Hill, N.C., 1972), pp. 7-27.
14. Ernest A. Baker, *The History of the English Novel* (London, 1935), 6: 135-38.
15. Louis D. Rubin, Jr., *The Writer in the South: Studies in a Literary Community* (Athens, Ga., 1972); Lewis P. Simpson, "The Southern Novelist and Southern Nationalism" and "The Southern Writer and the Great Literary Secession," both in his *The Man of Letters in New England and the South* (Baton Rouge, La., 1973), pp. 201-55.
16. "Ode to the Confederate Dead," lines 1-2, 44-50.
17. Ellen Glasgow, *The Woman Within* (New York, 1954), p. 129.
18. Ibid., p. 51.
19. Ellen Glasgow, *A Certain Measure: An Interpretation of Prose Fiction* (New York, 1943), p. 4.
20. *Certain Measure*, p. 3-5, 48-49, 66-72, and passim.
21. James Branch Cabell, *As I Remember It: Some Epilogues In Recollection* (New York, 1955), pp. 219-21.
22. See Daniel W. Patterson, "Ellen Glasgow's Plan for a Social History of Virginia," *Modern Fiction Studies* 5 (Winter 1959): 353-60; Oliver L. Steele, "Ellen Glasgow, Social History, and the 'Virginia Edition,'" *Modern Fiction Studies* 7 (Summer 1961): 173-76; Edgar E. MacDonald, "The Glasgow-Cabell Entente," *American Literature* 41 (March 1969): 76-91.
23. Judy Smith Murr, "History in *Barren Ground* and *Vein of Iron*: Theory, Structure, and Symbol," *Southern Literary Journal* 8 (Fall 1975): 39-54, despite its ostensible subject, does not deal with the issues of the relationship of history

Notes

and fiction; rather it deals with the synecdochical substitution of individual fictional lives for the larger sense of history.

24. *Certain Measure*, p. 181.
25. *Woman Within*, p. 104.
26. Ellen Glasgow, *The Battle-Ground*, Old Dominion Edition (Garden City, N.Y., 1929), p. vii.
27. *Certain Measure*, p. 12.
28. *Woman Within*, pp. 64, 38-40.
29. *Certain Measure*, p. 20.
30. *Woman Within*, p. 38.
31. Ibid., pp. 38-40, 64.
32. W. Gilmore Simms, *Mellichampe: A Legend of the Santee* (New York, 1853), p. 3.
33. [William Gilmore Simms], "Ellet's Women of the Revolution," *Southern Quarterly Review* 17 (1850): 351.
34. *Certain Measure*, p. 21; *The Battle-Ground*, Old Dominion Ed., p. viii.
35. *Certain Measure*, p. 21.
36. E. Stanly Godbold, Jr., *Ellen Glasgow and the Woman Within* (Baton Rouge, La., 1972), p. 59.
37. *Certain Measure*, p. 6.
38. Ibid., p. 21.
39. Ibid., p. 6.
40. Blair Rouse, ed., *Letters of Ellen Glasgow* (New York, 1958), p. 30.
41. *Certain Measure*, p. 19.
42. *The Battle-Ground*, Old Dominion Ed., p. viii.
43. Joan Foster Santas, in *Ellen Glasgow's American Dream* (Charlottesville, Va., 1965), p. 51, cites Thomas Nelson Page's picture of southern Unionists who fought in the Confederate Army, in *The Old Dominion: Her Making and Manners* (New York, 1908), pp. 240-41, as evidence of the accuracy of the portrayal of Peyton Ambler.
44. Joan Santas (p. 55) cites George W. Bagby's *The Old Virginia Gentleman and Other Sketches* (New York, 1910), on the accuracy of this view of how young Virginians went off to war.
45. *Certain Measure*, p. 13.
46. Ibid., p. 22.
47. *The Battle-Ground* (New York, 1902), pp. 442-43.
48. Ibid., pp. 478-79.
49. Ibid., p. 485.
50. In a speech before the Southern Writers Conference, cited in Godbold, p. 244.
51. *The Battle-Ground*, 1902 ed., pp. 492-93.
52. William Gilmore Simms, *The Yemassee*, ed. Alexander Cowie (New York, 1937), p. xxxix.
53. Stark Young, *So Red the Rose* (New York, 1953), p. 127.
54. Ibid., p. 383.
55. Ibid., pp. 150-51.
56. Louis Auchincloss, *Ellen Glasgow* (Minneapolis, Minn., 1964), p. 12; Julia Peterkin praised it in a review in the Washington *Post*, quoted on dust-jacket of 81st impression.
57. Allen Tate, *The Fathers* (Denver, Colo., 1960), pp. 267-68.
58. Ibid., p. 268.
59. Ibid., pp. 125-26.
60. Ibid., p. 117.

61. Examples of such novels are *Moby-Dick, The Blithedale Romance, My Ántonia, The Great Gatsby, You Can't Go Home Again,* and, in a special way, *Absalom, Absalom!*
62. Tate, p. 44.
63. Ibid., p. 153. Perhaps it is this carefully contrived carelessness about historical event that leads Tate to feel justified in his casuistical claim that *The Fathers* is not an historical novel.
64. See Eugene D. Genovese, *Roll Jordan Roll: The World the Slaves Made* (New York, 1975).
65. Margaret Mead, "Foreword" to *Life Is With People: The Culture of the Shtetl,* by Mark Zborowski and Elizabeth Herzog (New York, 1962), p. 11.
66. Glasgow, *A Certain Measure,* p. 66.

Chapter 4

To Grieve on Universal Bones

1. Robert Penn Warren, in *Fugitive's Reunion,* ed. Rob Roy Purdy (Nashville, Tenn., 1959), p. 210.
2. Arthur Mizener, "The Realistic Novel as Symbol," *The Sense of Life in the Modern Novel* (Boston, 1964), pp. 270, 287.
3. Ibid., pp. 268-69.
4. Allen Tate, "A Southern Mode of the Imagination," *Essays of Four Decades* (Chicago, 1968), p. 578.
5. "*The Sheltered Life* . . . is . . . the second favourite among my books. . . . after *Barren Ground* I like it best of my novels." Letter to Signe Toksvig, October 8, 1944, *Letters of Ellen Glasgow,* ed. Blair Rouse (New York, 1958), p. 354.
6. Ibid., p. 176, where she says, "My idea of a well-made book is *To the Lighthouse.*"
7. Ibid., p. 354.
8. Ellen Glasgow, *The Sheltered Life* (New York, 1932), p. 139.
9. Ibid., p. 150.
10. Ibid., p. 151.
11. Ibid., pp. 163-64.
12. William Faulkner, *Absalom, Absalom!* (New York, 1936), following p. 384. This map, redrawn and expanded, has been reproduced many times.
13. Steven Marcus, *Representations: Essays on Literature and Society* (New York, 1976), pp. xiii-xvii.
14. Mark Schorer, *Sinclair Lewis: An American Life* (New York, 1961), p. 813.
15. William Faulkner, *Light in August* (New York, 1932), p. 449.
16. Ibid., p. 467.
17. Ibid., pp. 466-67.
18. Ibid., p. 462.
19. *Absalom, Absalom!,* pp. 100-101.
20. *Faulkner at the University,* ed. Frederick Gwyn and Joseph L. Blotner (New York, 1965), p. 273.
21. Robert Penn Warren, *All the King's Men* (New York, 1946), p. 201.
22. Ibid., p. 200.
23. Ibid., p. 461, 464.
24. Robert Penn Warren, *World Enough and Time: A Romantic Novel* (New York, 1950), p. 3.
25. Robert Penn Warren, *Brother to Dragons: A Tale in Verse and Voices* (New

York, 1953), p. 192.

26. Walter Sullivan, "The Historical Novelist and the Existential Peril: Robert Penn Warren's *Band of Angels,*" in his *Death by Melancholy: Essays on Modern Southern Fiction* (Baton Rouge, La., 1972), pp. 36-51.

27. Robert Penn Warren, *Band of Angels* (New York, 1955), p. 3. Lest this be taken as Warren's personal position, see his *Democracy and Poetry* (Cambridge, Mass., 1975), throughout, but particularly p. xii.

28. Robert Penn Warren, *Wilderness: A Tale of the Civil War* (New York, 1961), p. 225.

29. Ibid., pp. 69, 73, 77, 78.

30. William Styron, *The Confessions of Nat Turner* (New York, 1967), p. [ix].

31. John Henrik Clarke, ed., *William Styron's Nat Turner: Ten Black Writers Respond* (Boston, 1968).

32. Tate, "The Profession of Letters in the South," *Essays,* pp. 533-34.

33. Tate, "A Southern Mode of the Imagination," *Essays,* p. 582.

34. *All the King's Men,* p. 464.

Chapter 5

"The Cosmic Clock of History"

1. Karl Mannheim, *Essays on the Sociology of Knowledge* (New York, 1952), p. 84; Edwin Muir, *The Structure of the Novel* (London, 1957), p. 63; Warren, *Democracy and Poetry,* p. 54. It should be noted that Muir's perceptive distinction between time and space in the novel (pp. 62-114) is made to define fictional genera rather than philosophical stances.

2. Charles Olson, *Call Me Ishmael* (New York, 1947), p. 11. See also pp. 114-19, where Olson elaborates on this apperception.

3. Joseph Frank, "Spatial Form in Modern Literature," in *Criticism: The Foundations of Modern Literary Judgment,* ed. Mark Schorer, Josephine Miles, and Gordon McKenzie (New York, 1948), p. 392. This is the author's revision of an essay originally published in *Sewanee Review* 53 (1945): 221-40, 433-56, 643-53. All future references are to the revised version in *Criticism,* pp. 379-92.

4. Randall Stewart, "Hawthorne and Faulkner," *College English* 17 (February 1956): pp. 257-62; Stewart, *American Literature and Christian Doctrine* (Baton Rouge, La., 1958), p. 138; William Van O'Connor, "Hawthorne and Faulkner: Some Common Ground," *Virginia Quarterly Review* 33 (Winter 1957): 105-23.

5. Notably in F. O. Matthiessen, *American Renaissance: Art and Expression in the Age of Emerson and Whitman* (New York, 1941), pp. 275-91.

6. Steven Marcus, "Literature and Society: Starting In with George Eliot," *Representations: Essays on Literature and Society* (New York, 1975), p. 183.

7. "With the partial exception of the Old South . . . Americans in general have had to do without the kind of inherited cultural history that many Europeans have enjoyed," says Marcus, "Awakening from the Nightmare? Notes on the Historical Novel," *Representations,* p. 168.

8. Richard Chase, *The American Novel and Its Tradition* (Garden City, N.Y., 1957).

9. Philip Rahv, "The Myth and the Powerhouse," *Literature and the Sixth Sense* (Boston, 1969), p. 210.

10. F. Garvin Davenport, Jr., *The Myth of Southern History: Historical Consciousness in Twentieth-Century Southern Literature* (Nashville, Tenn., 1970), pp. 8-43; Wilbur J. Cash, *The Mind of the South* (New York, 1941).

11. Mircea Eliade, *Cosmos and History: The Myth of the Eternal Return* (New York, 1959).
12. Lewis P. Simpson, *The Dispossessed Garden: Pastoral and History in Southern Literature* (Athens, Ga., 1975); Walter Sullivan, *A Requiem for the Renascence: The State of Fiction in the Modern South* (Athens, Ga., 1976). Both critics acknowledge a deep debt to Eric Voegelin's studies of history.
13. Robert Penn Warren, *Segregation: The Inner Conflict of the South* (New York, 1957), p. 15; see also Virginia Rock, "Agrarianism as a Theme in Southern Literature: The Period Since 1925," *Georgia Review* 11 (Summer 1957): 154-60.
14. Andrew Lytle, "The Working Novelist and the Mythmaking Process," *The Hero with the Private Parts* (Baton Rouge, La., 1966), p. 189.
15. Thomas Wolfe, *Look Homeward, Angel* (New York, 1929), pp. 192, 49, 70.
16. Thomas Wolfe, *The Story of a Novel* (New York, 1936), pp. 51-52. Cf. James Joyce's remark to Eugene Jolas, about *Finnegans Wake,* "Time and the river and the mountain are the real heroes of my book," quoted in Richard Ellmann, *James Joyce* (New York, 1959), p. 565.
17. Frank, p. 367.
18. Margaret Church, *Time and Reality: Studies in Contemporary Fiction* (Chapel Hill, N.C., 1963), pp. 237-50.
19. Karl E. Zink, "Flux and the Frozen Moment: The Imagery of Stasis in Faulkner's Prose," *PMLA* 71 (June 1956): 285-301. See especially Richard P. Adams, *Faulkner: Myth and Motion* (Princeton, N.J., 1968).
20. Church, pp. 205-53.
21. Hans Meyerhoff, *Time in Literature* (Berkeley, Calif., 1960), pp. 16, 26, 41, 44, 53, 81.
22. Rahv, pp. 204-5.
23. Warren, *Democracy and Poetry*, p. 56.

A Note on Sources

THIS NOTE makes no attempt to be exhaustive, and it is designed primarily to indicate the principal sources which I have found particularly useful about the thesis I am developing. I have not listed works on individual authors unless they have been useful in developing the general themes.

On theories of history and the relation of history to literature, I have found the following works useful, although I do not always agree with them: Harvey Gross, *The Contrived Corridor: History and Fatality in Modern Literature* (1971); R. G. Collingwood, *The Idea of History* (1946); Reinhold Niebuhr, *The Irony of American History* (1952); G.W.F. Hegel, *The Philosophy of History*, trans. J. Sibree (1899); Friedrich Nietzsche, "The Use and Abuse of History," *Thoughts Out of Season*, trans. Adrian Collins (1909–1913); C. Vann Woodward, *The Burden of Southern History* (1960); Harry B. Henderson, III, *Versions of the Past: The Historical Imagination in American Fiction* (1974); Roy Harvey Pearce, *Historicism Once More: Problems and Occasions for the American Scholar* (1969); Philip Rahv, *Literature and the Sixth Sense* (1969); C. A. Patrides, ed., *Aspects of Time* (Manchester, England, 1976).

On the special forms of the novel, the following works have been useful. On historical fiction: George Lukács, *The Historical Novel*, trans. Hannah and Stanley Mitchell (1963); Avron Fleishman, *The English Historical Novel: Walter Scott to Virginia Woolf* (1971); David Levin, *In Defense of Historical Literature* (1967); Herbert Butterfield, *The Historical Novel: An Essay* (1924); Alfred T. Sheppard, *The Art and Practice of Historical Fiction* (1934); George Dekker, *James Fenimore Cooper, the Novelist* (1967); Ernest A. Baker, *History of the English Novel*, 6 (1934).

On the novel of manners: James W. Tuttleton, *The Novel of Manners in America* (1972); Louis Auchincloss, *Reflections of a*

Jacobite (1961); Arthur Mizener, *The Sense of Life in the Modern Novel* (1964); Steven Marcus, *Representations: Essays on Literature and Society* (1976); and Michael Millgate, *American Social Fiction: James to Cozzens* (1964).

Of the numerous studies of the South as a region the following have been particularly helpful: William R. Taylor, *Cavalier and Yankee: The Old South and American National Character* (1961); C. Vann Woodward, *Origins of the New South, 1877–1913* (1951) and *The Burden of Southern History* (1960); W. J. Cash, *The Mind of the South* (1941); Clement Eaton, *Freedom of Thought in the Old South* (1940), *The Mind of the Old South* (1967), *The Waning of the Old South Civilization 1860–1880's* (1968), and *The Growth of Southern Civilization, 1790–1860* (1961); Paul S. Buck, *The Road to Reunion, 1865–1900* (1937); Charles G. Sellers, Jr. (ed.), *The Southerner as American* (1960); James McBride Dabbs, *Who Speaks for the South?* (1964); Henry Savage, Jr., *Seeds of Time: The Background of Southern Thinking* (1959); Ben Robertson, *Red Hills and Cotton: An Upcountry Memory* (1942).

On southern literature and literary culture, the following books have been helpful: Jay B. Hubbell, *The South in American Literature 1607–1900* (1954); Edmund Wilson, *Patriotic Gore: Studies in the Literature of the Civil War* (1962); Louis D. Rubin, Jr., *The Faraway Country: Writers of the Modern South* (1963), *The Curious Death of the Novel* (1967), *The Writer in the South: Studies in a Literary Community* (1972), and *William Elliott Shoots a Bear: Essays on the Southern Literary Imagination* (1975); Lewis P. Simpson, *The Man of Letters in New England and the South: Essays on the History of the Literary Vocation in America* (1973) and *The Dispossessed Garden: Pastoral and History in Southern Literature* (1975); F. Garvin Davenport, Jr., *The Myth of Southern History: Historical Consciousness in Twentieth-Century Southern Literature* (1970); Walter Sullivan, *Death by Melancholy: Essays on Modern Southern Fiction* (1972); Robert A. Lively, *Fiction Fights the Civil War* (1957); Frederick J. Hoffman, *The Art of Southern Fiction* (1967); Walter Sullivan, *A Requiem for the Renascence* (1976).

For information about the American Revolutionary War, I have depended primarily on John C. Miller, *The Triumph of Freedom 1775–1783* (1948); Willard M. Wallace, *Appeal to Arms: A Military History of the American Revolution* (1951); John Richard Alden, *The American Revolution 1775–1783* (1954) and *The South in the Revolution 1763–1789* (1957); Paul H. Smith, *Loyalists and Redcoats: A Study in British Revolutionary Policy* (1964); C. H. Van Tine, *The Loyalists in the American Revolution*

(1902); Don Higginbotham, *The War of American Independence* (1971); Edward McCrady, *The History of South Carolina in the Revolution, 1780–1783* (1902); Wallace Brown, *The Good Americans: The Loyalists in the American Revolution* (1969).

About the Civil War, I have depended primarily on E. Merton Coulter, *The Confederate States of America 1861–1865* (1950); David M. Potter, *The Impending Crisis 1848–1861* (1976); Shelby Foote, *The Civil War: A Narrative* (1958–1974); and Bruce Catton, *The Centennial History of the Civil War.*

I have found valuable Eugene D. Genovese, *The World the Slaveholders Made* (1969) and *Roll, Jordan, Roll: The World the Slaves Made* (1975); Kenneth Stampp, *The Peculiar Institution: Slavery in the Ante-Bellum South* (1956); Robert William Fogle and Stanley L. Engerman, *Time on the Cross: The Economics of American Negro Slavery* (1974); William W. Freehling, *Prelude to Civil War: The Nullification Controversy in South Carolina, 1816–1836* (1966); and Louis B. Wright's charming *South Carolina: A Bicentennial History* (1976).

Index

This index contains the names of persons and titles appearing in the text proper. It does not list subjects, footnote references, or items from "A Note on Sources."

Aaron, Daniel, 39
Absalom, Absalom! (Faulkner), 47, 59, 72, 75–78, 81, 82
Ainsworth, Harrison, 9
All the King's Men (Warren), 2, 79–81, 85, 92
American Loyalist, The (Sabine), 22, 23
American Novel and Its Tradition, The (Chase), 95
At the Moon's Inn (Lytle), 90

Bacon, Nathaniel, Jr., 37
Baker, Ernest A., 44
Baldwin, Joseph Glover, 34
"Ballad of Billie Potts, The," (Warren), 81
Bancroft, George, 25
Band of Angels (Warren), 84–85
Battle-Ground, The (Glasgow), 46–54, 62
"Bear, The" (Faulkner), 9, 91
Beauchamp-Sharp murder case, 81
Bellow, Saul, 2
Bergson, Henri, 100
Border Beagles (Simms), 18
Boyd, James, 37
Bristow, Gwen, 64
Brother to Dragons (Warren), 38, 83–84, 85
Byrd, William, 3

Cabell, James Branch, 45, 46, 68
Call Me Ishmael (Olson), 94
Caruthers, William Alexander, 37
Cassique of Kiawah, The (Simms), 20
Cather, Willa, 63
Cavaliers of Virginia, The (Caruthers), 37
Cease Firing (Johnston), 39

Certain Measure, A (Glasgow), 45
Chase, Richard, 95
Chesnut, Mrs. Mary, 39
"Chickamauga" (Wolfe), 99
Church, Margaret, 100
Clansman, The (Dixon), 42
Clemens, Samuel Langhorne, 9
Clinton, Sir Henry, 25
Coleridge, Samuel Taylor, 8
Confessions of Nat Turner, The (Styron), 10, 89–90
Cooke, John Esten, 37, 39
Cooper, James Fenimore, 8, 15, 48
Cornwallis, Lord Charles, 28
Crane, Stephen, 50

Davidson, Donald, 18, 69
Davis, Richard Beale, 10
De Bow's Review, 13
Deliverance, The (Glasgow), 54
Die Räuber (Schiller), 31
Dispossessed Garden, The (Simpson), 96
Dixon, Thomas, Jr., 42
Doctor Faustus (Marlowe), 91
Drums (Boyd), 37

Eliade, Mircea, 96
Ellison, Ralph, 8, 69
Emerson, Ralph Waldo, 5
"Epochs and Events of American History, as Suited to the Purposes of Art in Fiction, The" (Simms), 21
Erskine, John, 23
Essay on Calcareous Manures, An (Ruffin), 9
Essays on the Sociology of Knowledge (Mannheim), 93
Eutaw (Simms), 19, 20, 32, 33, 35

115

Fable, A (Faulkner), 99
Falkner, William C., 73
Fathers, The (Tate), 59–62, 67
Faulkner, William, 1, 9, 59, 72–79, 91, 99–100
Fiction Fights the Civil War (Lively), 40
Fitzgerald, F. Scott, 2, 68, 100
Fletcher, Inglis, 64
Flush Times of Alabama and Mississippi, The (Baldwin), 34
Foote, Shelby, 57
Forayers, The (Simms), 19, 32, 33, 35
Ford, Jesse Hill, 64
Forge, The (Stribling), 90
Fugitives' Reunion, 66

Gadsden, Christopher, 17
Gates, Mrs. Jacob, 16
Genovese, Eugene D., 62
Georgia Scenes (Longstreet), 34
Glasgow, Ellen, 45–56, 59, 64, 67, 68, 70–72, 73, 80, 100
Gone With the Wind (Mitchell), 58–59, 62
Gordon, Caroline, 64, 68, 90
Great Gatsby, The (Fitzgerald), 2
Great Meadow, The (Roberts), 90
Green Centuries (Gordon), 64, 90
Greene, Nathanael, 17, 24, 28, 35
Griswold, Rufus W., 17

Hardy, Thomas, 71
Harris, George Washington, 34
Hawthorne, Nathaniel, 8, 67, 94–95
Hegel, Georg Wilhelm Friedrich, 4, 5, 6, 7, 14, 27, 41, 92, 93, 100, 101
Hemingway, Ernest, 68
Henry Esmond (Thackeray), 19
Henry St. John, Gentleman (Cooke), 37
Hero with the Private Parts, The (Lytle), 97
Heyward, DuBose, 45, 56, 59, 67
Hills Beyond, The (Wolfe), 98
Hilt to Hilt (Cooke), 37, 39
History of South Carolina, The (Simms), 17, 29
Hoffman, Charles Fenno, 81
Horse-Shoe Robinson (Kennedy), 23, 37
Huger, Isaac, 17
Huxley, Aldous, 100

In Ole Virginia (Page), 42
Intruder in the Dust (Faulkner), 1

Jackson, Thomas (Stonewall), 51
James, G.P.R., 9
James, Henry, 67
Jefferson, Thomas, 10, 38, 83
Johnston, Mary, 37, 90
Joscelyn: A Tale of the Revolution (Simms), 20
Joyce, James, 100
Jubilee (Walker), 62–63
Jung, Carl, 96

Kafka, Franz, 100
Katharine Walton (Simms), 19, 24, 30
Kennedy, John Pendleton, 23, 37
Killer Angels, The (Shaara), 37
Kinsmen, The (Simms), 18
Knights of the Horse Shoe, The (Caruthers), 37
Kosciusko, Thadeusz, 17

Lanier, Sidney, 39
Leather Stocking and Silk (Cooke), 37
Leatherstocking Tales (Cooper), 15
Lee, Charles, 17
Legacy of the Civil War, The (Warren), 86
Leopard's Spots, The (Dixon), 42
Lewis, Sinclair, 73
Life of Francis Marion, The (Simms), 17
Life of Nathanael Greene, The (Simms), 17
Light in August (Faulkner), 73–75
Lincoln, Benjamin, 25
Lionel Lincoln (Cooper), 8
Lively, Robert A., 40
Long Hunt (Boyd), 37
Long Night, The (Lytle), 90
Long Roll, The (Johnston), 39
Longstreet, Augustus Baldwin, 34
Look Homeward, Angel (Wolfe), 98
Lowell, James Russell, 6
Lukács, Georg, 7, 27
Lytle, Andrew, 90, 97

McClellen, George, 50
McCrady, Edward, 29
Mann, Thomas, 100
Mannheim, Karl, 93

Index

Marching On (Boyd), 37
Marcus, Steven, 73, 95
Marion, Francis, 18, 24, 26, 27, 31, 32
Mark Twain. *See* Clemens, Samuel Langhorne
Marx, Karl, 5
"Massachusetts to Virginia" (Whittier), 21
Mead, Margaret, 63
Mellichampe (Simms), 16, 18, 23, 24, 29, 30
Melville, Herman, 94, 95
Merry Wives of Windsor, The (Shakespeare), 31
Meyerhoff, Hans, 100
Miller, John C., 26
Mitchell, Margaret, 45, 58-59, 67
Mizener, Arthur, 67, 68
Moby-Dick (Melville), 94
Mohun (Cooke), 37, 39
Moultrie, William, 17
Muir, Edwin, 93

New York *Herald*, 48
Niebuhr, Reinhold, 4
Nietzsche, Friedrich, 6, 7, 15, 41, 93, 96, 100, 101
None Shall Look Back (Gordon), 64, 90

O'Connor, Flannery, 69
"Ode to the Confederate Dead" (Tate), 44
Old Gentleman of the Black Stock, The (Page), 42
Old Guard Magazine, 20
Olson, Charles, 94

Page, Thomas Nelson, 42
Page, Walter Hines, 49
Partisan, The (Simms), 16, 18, 23, 24, 29, 30, 32
Peter Ashley (Heyward), 56, 59
Peterkin, Julia, 59
Philosophy of History, The (Hegel), 4
Pickens, Andrew, 26
Pinckney, Charles Cotesworth, 17
Pioneers, The (Cooper), 48
Poe, Edgar Allan, 81
Porter, Katherine Anne, 68
Proust, Marcel, 99, 100

Rahv, Philip, 95-96, 100
Raider, The (Ford), 64
Ransom, John Crowe, 69
Rawdon, Lord Francis, 28
Rawlings, Virginia, 47
Red Badge of Courage, The (Crane), 50
Red Rock (Page), 42
Requiem for a Nun (Faulkner), 72
Requiem for the Renascence, A (Sullivan), 96
Richard Hurdis (Simms), 18
Richmond (Va.) *Enquirer*, 48
Richmond (Va.) *Examiner*, 48
Roberts, Elizabeth Madox, 90
Rob of the Bowl (Kennedy), 37
Romance of a Plain Man, The (Glasgow), 55
Rubin, Louis D., Jr., 40
Ruffin, Edmund, 9

Sabine, Lorenzo, 22
Sartre, Jean-Paul, 100
Scarlet Letter, The (Hawthorne), 67, 94-95
Schiller, Johann Friedrich von, 31
Schorer, Mark, 73
Scott, Evelyn, 90
Scott, Sir Walter, 7, 8, 9, 10, 12, 19, 21, 27, 28, 36, 37, 39, 44, 45, 66, 67, 95, 100
Scout, The (Simms), 18, 23, 24, 29, 30, 31
Segregation: The Inner Conflict of the South (Warren), 86
Shaara, Michael, 37
Shakespeare, William, 31, 91
Sheltered Life, The (Glasgow), 70-72, 73, 80, 100
Sherman, William Tecumseh, 57
Simms, William Gilmore, 13-36, 47, 56, 64, 66, 81, 90
Simms's Magazine, 23
Simpson, Lewis, 96
Soldier's Pay (Faulkner), 19
So Red the Rose (Young), 13, 56-58, 59, 62
Sound and the Fury, The (Faulkner), 78
South Carolina in the Revolutionary War (Simms), 17, 22
Southern and Western Magazine, 23
Spotswood, Alexander, 37
Store, The (Stribling), 90

Story of a Novel, The (Wolfe), 99
Stowe, Harriet Beecher, 84
Stribling, T. S., 90
Structure of the Novel, The (Muir), 93
Styron, William, 8, 10, 88–90
Sullivan, Walter, 84–85, 96
Sumter, Thomas, 17, 24, 26, 27
Surry of Eagle's-Nest (Cooke), 37, 39
Sut Lovingood Yarns (Harris), 34
Sword and the Distaff, The (Simms), 19

Tate, Allen, 44, 45, 59–62, 67, 68
Taylor, William R., 14, 15, 27
Taylor, Zachary, 23
Thackeray, William Makepeace, 19, 37, 45, 59
Thoreau, Henry David, 6
Tiger-Lilies (Lanier), 39
Time and Reality (Church), 100
Time in Literature (Meyerhoff), 100
Time of Man, The (Roberts), 90
To the Lighthouse (Woolf), 70
Toynbee, Arnold J., 40
Tri-Color, or the Three Days of Blood in Paris, The (Simms), 20–21
Twain, Mark. *See* Clemens, Samuel Langhorne

Uncle Tom's Cabin (Stowe), 84, 90–91
Unfinished Cathedral (Stribling), 90

Vauthier, Simone, 14, 17
Velvet Horn, The (Lytle), 90, 97

Virginia Comedians, The (Cooke), 37
Voice of the People, The (Glasgow), 54

Walker, Margaret, 45, 62–63, 67
Warren, Lella, 64
Warren, Robert Penn, 1, 2, 8, 38, 66, 68 79–87, 92, 93, 96, 101
Washington and the Generals of the American Revolution (Griswold), 17
Wave, The (Scott), 90
Waverley (Scott), 19
Waverley Novels (Scott), 7, 8, 9, 27
"Web of Earth, The" (Wolfe), 99
Welty, Eudora, 68
Wharton, Edith, 43
White Rose of Memphis, The (Falkner), 73
Whittier, John Greenleaf, 21
Who Speaks for the Negro? (Warren), 86
Wilderness (Warren), 86–87
Williams, Otho H., 26
Williams, Tennessee, 68
Wolfe, Thomas, 68, 98–*100*
Woodcraft (Simms), 19, 31
Woodward, C. Vann, 8, 41
Woolf, Virginia, 70, 72, 100
World Enough and Time (Warren), 1, 81–83, 85
Wright, Louis B., 3

Young, Stark, 13, 45, 56–58, 59, 67, 68

www.ingramcontent.com/pod-product-compliance
Lightning Source LLC
Chambersburg PA
CBHW020806160426
43192CB00006B/461